PLAYBUILDING

Dedicated to all those who created Shopfront.

Acknowledgments: Thanks to Shopfront Theatre For Young People for making all their records and facilities available. Special thanks to Shopfront's Artistic Director, John du Feu, for his helpful comments and corrections as the book was written. Thanks to Michael Curnick for finding and providing the photographs. Thanks for helping reconstruct various scenarios to Andrew Brook; Luke Tebbutt; David Malek; Alice Moore; Liz Hill; Martin Blacker; Francine Sparre; Kris Plummer.

PLAYBUILDING

ERROL BRAY

HEINEMANN • PORTSMOUTH, NH

Heinemann
A division of Reed Elsevier Inc.
361 Hanover Street
Portsmouth, NH 03801
Offices and agents throughout the world

This edition is not for sale in Australia, New Zealand, the UK or Europe.
Distributed in Canada by Reed Books Canada, 75 Clegg Road,
Markham, Ontario L6G 1A1

Library of Congress Cataloging-in-Publication Data
Bray, Errol
Playbuilding: a guide to group creation of plays
with young people.

ISBN 0-435-08635-9
1.Drama - Study and teaching. I. Title
792.07

First published by Currency Press, Australia
Printed by Southwood Press, Sydney, Australia

CONTENTS

INTRODUCTION

Playbuilding is an exciting theatre technique for creating plays and performances with groups. This type of group and co-operative creation has become more and more accepted as an effective theatre form and is especially popular with directors and teachers who work with young people. This is a handbook for playbuilders with special emphasis on working with young people in schools or youth arts groups. You will find step-by-step instructions on playbuilding techniques alongside notes on attitudes and philosophies behind the idea of playbuilding. You will also find detailed descriptions of projects that I have completed with young people, in a number of different work situations.

Playbuilding is a dynamic and interactive process that draws out individual creativity very intensely while also developing strong group co-operation and commitment. It allows people, whatever their talent, to be immediately involved in a richly creative process. This process offers each participant the fullest and most satisfying involvement in drama that is possible. It is very much a hands-on process which requires an imaginative, flexible director committed to the creative development of the group. Playbuilding enables a participant to come to grips with the pleasures and problems of every aspect of drama and theatre; to be playwright, performer, director, composer, technician, designer, critic. It introduces participants to the creative discipline and co-operation required in theatre. It opens up exciting possibilities for learning, skill development, expression, personal enrichment, and fun.

The term playbuilding is used to describe the creative process of assembling a dramatic performance or presentation from the building blocks of drama and theatre, through improvisation, discussion and rehearsal. The process involves rehearsing the play as it is created, thus developing a strong presentation that comes to belong to the group in a very personal and committed way. Improvisations are analysed, reshaped and refined in the ongoing workshops. Ideas, written material, found material; all are selected for inclusion in the play through a rigorous discussion process. Because the play is rehearsed constantly as each scene is created and added, the performance skills and confidence of the group rapidly become polished and strong. All types of plays for groups of all sizes and ages can be forged through the playbuilding process — realistic dramas; episodic theme-plays; musicals; documentaries; epic theatre; narrative theatre; adaptations of literature; revues; dance dramas; television plays; and more. Playbuilding deals simultaneously with the physical, intellectual, social and creative skills of the group. It helps develop imagination, analytic and structuring abilities, co-operation, theatre talent, confidence, communication skills and a sense of commitment in each member of the group.

Many adults have seemed surprised over the years that so many boys have been very actively involved in Playbuilding. Apparently, drama is supposed to be an activity for girls and is an activity that boys will think is not masculine enough for them. All this is nonsense, of course, and only exists while people treat theatre and creative work as something rather falsely precious and arty. It is imperative that people working with kids promote the idea that creative work is work and that it is a basic part of everyone's life. Creative people are not weird or different, because everyone is creative. You hammer out a play in just the same way as you would hammer out a cubbyhouse. The guidelines for achieving successful playbuilding are straightforward and quite matter-of-fact. It simply involves unlocking people's imaginations and handing them creative tools for construction.

BACKGROUND TO THE GUIDELINES

I have developed the techniques of playbuilding outlined in this book over fifteen years of work in schools, youth arts organisations and especially at the Shopfront Theatre For Young People in Sydney. The techniques are thoroughly tried and tested, having been used by me to create over fifty major productions as well as in numerous one-off workshops and teacher-training sessions. This work has covered a broad range — plays on specific school subjects such as Captain Cook; the book of *The Hobbit*; romance literature with emphasis on *Romeo and Juliet*; skill development projects for performers and young writers; plays on social issues such as lone parents, peer pressure, drugs, peace; television segments on specific educational issues for the ABC.; Theatre-in-Education plays for touring to schools; plays for community, national and international festivals; music-based dramas; documentary-style plays using material researched by the participants; bizarre, fun plays centred in sheer entertainment and celebration.

My early work was in schools around Sydney and some of that work, in a 'tough' inner-city school, was toured by the Education Department to other schools as a way of encouraging teachers to do more drama in class. I was co-founder of Shopfront Theatre For Young People and its Artistic Director for almost nine years. In that time the exciting work created by Shopfront kids drew more and more acclaim and became accepted and supported at the community level with real passion. Shopfront also developed an international reputation for innovative, high standard theatre. All the plays I helped create at Shopfront were shown in seasons for community audiences; some were televised nationally; some toured to schools with the Shopfront Theatre-in-Education teams; five were toured overseas. One of the plays detailed in this book — *Piece by Piece* on the theme of peace — was invited to an International Youth Festival in Canada where it received a standing ovation at every performance and then went on to perform at the United Nations in New York. All the work at Shopfront was based in the playbuilding techniques and attitudes outlined in this book. Shopfront's reputation and success demonstrate the power and quality available to ordinary young people through playbuilding. Most importantly, Shopfront has given its young people, through play-building, a strong, theatrical 'voice' that is constantly entertaining and thought-provoking.

Errol Bray
Sydney, 1991

PART ONE

PLAYBUILDING TECHNIQUE

Penguin and the lion scene, *Piece by Piece*.

CHAPTER I

STARTING POINTS

1 12

There are four broad areas that I offer to groups when we look at how we will go about creating our play: Theme; Story; Character; Setting. Discussion of these can often help narrow the group's area of search for an idea. Many groups and their directors are drawn to plot or character starting points because these are the most common types of drama seen on stage or on TV. But these are the plays that writers can deal with most effectively. The dramatic problems they present are the kind that require a strong writer or actor to solve, rather than the group strengths that effective playbuilding thrives upon.

This is not to discourage a group from ever attempting story or character starting points, but I would usually only encourage experienced groups to attempt these because they are more difficult and offer a developmental step in playbuilding skill. For a beginners' group I have found the theme to be the most effective way to build a play that will satisfy all the group. The Theme Play is effective in a wide variety of situations, enabling more scope for participants than most other methods.

No play will ever fall entirely into just one category. A good Theme Play will have strong story, character and setting elements in many scenes. A Character Play often needs a good plot line. A play that concentrates on setting may also have rich characterisations. Not all topics fit snugly into expectations. When I did a play with Primary students about Captain Cook — a topic they were studying at school — it became much more a Setting Play than a Character Play because the kids were concerned to talk about the changes that had occurred around Botany Bay since Cook's visit. The character of Cook was not explored at all and he became a device for talking about the city's modern life.

It is important for the director to identify the area within which the play is developing so that appropriate drama and theatre techniques can be applied. But it is also important to remain flexible and not to close off dramatic possibilities. In the case of *Having a Captain Cook* I knew where to encourage and push the group once it was clear that they were most keen on a Setting Play. But if the student playing the role of Cook had wanted to develop the characterisation I would have ensured that this interest was absorbed into the play. Having a group decision on the play's direction — and in this case on its title also — gave me clear guidelines on: the material most appropriate to the play; how to direct discussion; how to adjudicate on which scene-ideas to follow up; how much effort had to be given to set and costume creation; how much research was needed; how to structure the play.

Guidelines are important for the director so that you can keep the commitment from the group clear and alive; and to enable you to choose rationally from the bombardment of ideas and suggestions. Most plays have to be limited in length — most playbuilt shows seem to run from forty to sixty minutes — so the editing process must occur from the very start of a project. Any guidelines that the group can agree upon are valuable to the director. They can be used to justify almost all decisions about what goes into the play; and provide an objective means of discarding a good idea when it does not fit the criteria. The agreed guidelines give the director the security of always being able to refer back to the dramatic needs of the project, the needs agreed upon by the group in open discussion.

THE THEME PLAY

I use this title to refer to plays that have some general topic — heroism, parents, peace, suicide, being thirteen — as the main structural thread of the play. The play will be episodic in structure and can include dramatic scenes, songs, dances, poems, monologues, mime, and, in fact, almost any element of dramatic presentation produced by the group. It is this episodic structure that most characterises the Theme Play in playbuilding, and its major advantage is that it gives every person in the group the chance to display their thinking and performing abilities to their fullest without making anyone take a back-seat for the whole play. The variety of material in a Theme Play gives an exciting energy to it.

Most scenes in a Theme Play are quite brief and will range from short points or jokes — perhaps only a few seconds long — to detailed scenes with their own plots, characters and settings which can be up to ten or twelve minutes long. This means that each scene is easily controlled by the participants and each scene can be polished and closely analysed more easily than can happen with a major story-line play, for example. Each piece of drama comes in compact form, not too daunting to young people but big enough to allow all the dramatic and theatrical strength of a group to be applied. Each scene can become rich and complex in dramatic detail and can become strong and subtle in theatrical presentation.

Short scenes help draw stronger commitment from the group to the whole play because every scene has its own gang of creators and performers who bring an intense commitment that comes from having their idea in the play and their special performance moment in the show. The variety of scenes gives everyone a chance to lead and to support in performance and the co-operation in the group grows from this. Discovering the way a wide range of ideas and approaches can blend together into a strong group statement brings depth of co-operation. The variety also enables the natural clowns to be funny and the serious-minded to be as serious as they like.

The episodic approach permits use of any special abilities group members may have. If someone can tap-dance then there can be a tap scene; musical kids can play or sing; those who want to write can write a scene or speech; juggling, mask-making, puppetry, almost any skill can be included. This approach also allows the director to encourage development of specific skills. For example, a neat theatrical view of how the economy works may be demonstrated by juggling balls and other objects, so everyone needs to learn juggling.

Having a collection of brief scenes ready to assemble as a Theme Play enables the group and director to challenge and manipulate the audience response. Anger can be followed by humour or tenderness; abstract presentation can be followed by a true-to-life scene; a song can be followed by a mime. A tragic scene can have enormous impact if it has been preceded by three hilarious scenes on the same theme. These quick mood shifts can give the Theme Play great energy and power. The power to provoke thought and to entertain comes from the quality of the ideas rather than from sustained acting or theatrical ability. It isn't so hard to be a strong performer for five minutes but very hard for a twelve-year-old to hold a consistent characterisation for an hour or to sustain a clear story-line through a whole play.

These strengths of the Theme Play make it my favourite way of working with young people in playbuilding. There are also problems, of course. The major difficulty is finding a structure for the play that is fully effective for the topic and the material. Chapter Six is devoted to that. Convincing young people that all these weird little pieces of ideas can actually turn into a play is sometimes difficult and can undermine commitment. Chapter Four has some ways of overcoming this.

Two kinds of play come up quite regularly — the Documentary Play and the Compilation Play. Both operate largely by the same rules that apply to the Theme play, though both are rather easier to create as their material is already given. Both require a lot of discussion about what material to include and how to structure the material chosen. This can make them very useful for teaching study and research methods, but problems of becoming a bit stodgy and obvious can arise and clever structuring is necessary.

I did a Theatre-in-Education play, called *The Shakespeare Show,* which we used to introduce students to a variety and scope of Shakespeare's work. All the material was from Shakespeare's plays and sonnets; even the answers to the interview questions put to Bill himself by the Elizabethan Broadcasting Corporation were quotes. This play required a lot of surprising devices — as well as occasional bursts of solid acting — to sell Shakespeare to rather reluctant audiences.

If advanced students are looking for a greater challenge then you may want to encourage involvement in a Character Play or a Story Play, or simply allow the scenes in their Theme Play to expand to the point where they feel satisfied. It is quite possible for a particularly good and important scene in a Theme Play to become the entire play through the discussions and workshops. There should be no closed doors and the director should be alert, observant and ready for all possibilities.

THE STORY PLAY

This type of project relies on plot as the main thread of the work. Early work would be based in discussion and story-line development rather than in improvisation. It is not necessary to have an airtight plot before the improvisations can begin, but a substantial amount of story needs to be there to enable effective improvising to occur. It is advisable to leave room for new and unexpected plot developments to occur in workshops. It is also a good idea to look at secondary and parallel plot developments later in the workshops. This leeway keeps alive an atmosphere of creative interest and commitment to the process.

There is not much room for chaos in playbuilding the Story Play, if you want the play to be coherent. The Theme Play often seems to thrive on chaos. Story Plays demand precision and careful planning, and continual testing of the strength of their basic thread, the plot, which must stand up to rigorous examination. The Story Play provides tighter boundaries than the Theme Play and the plot very much dictates what characters and settings can be used. The demand for dramatic discipline is an important element. This discipline must come early in the project for the backbone of the play is created first, i.e. the plot. In a Theme Play the backbone is created almost last for it is only after all the scenes are gathered that the final structure can be devised. So there is a certainty and strength immediately in a Story Play that comes from this early backbone creation.

All these qualities can make the Story Play an excellent choice for the smaller, more advanced group and for older students who already have some performance experience and some knowledge of theatre. It encourages a deep examination of cause-and-effect drama; of human motivations and character; of historical and creative comparisons with the group's story; of probability and possibility in the scheme of events; of inevitability. The Story Play has classic drama connections for its drive is the large action of the ancient Greek dramas.

The Story Play lends itself to a popular offshoot: The Quest Play, and an example is *S. K. Y.*, at the end of this chapter. This form can be a very useful way to create a story for the logic and drive is easily maintained, and quests can easily accommodate a wide variety of scenes and characters, making it easier to use all the group in significant roles. In many Story Plays the story necessarily centres on a small number of characters and this usually means that a lot of the group may lose some of their excitement and commitment. The Quest Play helps solve some of those problems and also offers an immediate sense of adventure. A Quest Play can also offer more bizarre twists to the plot than an ordinary story usually offers.

For the Year of the Child I created a play with a small group to tour Primary Schools, called *Quest for the IYC.* The 'IYC' was the rather pedantic United Nations Bill of Children's Rights about which our group felt it was important for kids to know. So our Quest Play led them excitingly towards this mysterious object with an array of weird and interesting characters along the way, including comic-book heroes, traditional fairy-tale characters, a couple of odd baddies, an aboriginal story-teller, a dancer. All these characters illustrated different concepts included in the Charter but, unlike the Charter itself, they were able to be funny and exaggerated, as well as serious. By the time the Charter was read out, the audience was prepared to absorb it and it had been given a dramatic importance through the process of the search that a mere reading could not bring to it.

THE CHARACTER PLAY

This is a popular first choice by groups too, but often for misguided reasons. They may want to use some TV hero or to send up their teachers. So the first step is to explain the difference between character and caricature. When send-ups or copying of characters is the main aim of the group, the life of the project will be very limited.

Caricature can be quite a rewarding area of playbuilding if easy options are avoided. Cardboard cut-outs don't take very long to create and that is easy work. But the group must then be ready to work hard on the satire of the play to ensure it stands up to scrutiny. With cardboard characters an audience is not engaged emotionally, except by the issues, which then come under more intense scrutiny. There is always an excitement in creating genuine satire, and clever caricature is fun too. Both require hard work and careful dramatic balance which is usually best achieved by experienced playbuilders. It is not advisable to throw beginners into such difficult work.

I created a play with a mixed-age group using caricatures — *The Twins versus General Injustice* (see Chapter Three). This project began as a rather simple attack on various social ills which were popular targets at the time. General Injustice, in army great-coat and battle-helmet, represented all the evils done to ordinary people. The Twins represented pure goodness and the liberation groups who were fighting for social justice. It didn't take long to realise that such a concept had little to say if confined to the basic characteristics of our protagonists. Some early scene creation ended up saying nothing challenging and nothing entertaining. We soon learned that we had to examine every aspect of our assumptions and that meant that the liberation groups came in for criticism and satire, as much as the forces of social oppression did. We agreed to turn all the assumptions on their heads and so ended up with a bizarre play that disturbed audiences and created lots of discussion. It was also very funny because the attitudes of the main characters remained fixed and transparent throughout the contortions of the plot.

Almost inevitably, General Injustice became something of a cult figure at Shopfront and ended up in several other plays. Being able to identify instantly what a character like General Injustice stands for can be very useful to a play. But cardboard characters never work in cardboard plays. A play has to offer something of real substance to its audience and if there is no substance in the characters, it has to be there in abundance in the other elements of the play.

The genuine Character Play in which the group attempts thoughtful portrayals of characters — real people known to them or composite characters — can provide a rewarding project. It is again one that I would discourage a first-time group from trying, but is very useful for groups who have developed their playbuilding skills and are looking for a challenge.

The Character Play requires precision and careful construction in creating its characters, but these do not provide as strong a backbone to the play as work on plot does. The character elements will still have to be threaded into a structure after their creation. This can often mean long discussion sessions to achieve a play framework for the characters, though improvisations with close analysis can also be used. If a group is adventurous and not too worried about having little direction in the first several workshops, it is preferable to keep working through improvisations because the work then takes on emotional qualities not really present in discussion.

Most Character Plays will need a plot and naturalistic performances to sustain the dramatic needs of the project, but there is always room for real experiment with the form. Character analysis can be presented to an audience in structures that do not include plot and in styles that involve direct address, episodic structure, songs, dance, poetry, and so on. Care must be taken that a plotless Character Play does not fizzle out, leaving the audience unsatisfied.

Character Plays should examine a number of characters. Encourage the group to give detailed attention to more than one character, otherwise you may find that only one performer gets much benefit from the project. Dramatically, character traits are most interesting when shown in interaction with other characters. Subtlety and shading of characters; contradictions and paradoxes; emotional control and emotional outbursts; all offer exciting elements of the Character Play and all appear at their best when included in a dramatic weaving of characters. The richer the characterisations, the less complex the plot need be. There is a temptation amongst young people to believe that Character Plays must have soap-opera plots of mind-boggling complexity. The opposite is true. The director must ensure that the work emphasis in the Character Play is on creation of complex characters who are believable and who engage our emotions. Simple goodies and baddies are only useful for satire, epics and soap-opera and do not offer as much challenge to a group as characterisation.

As with all the classifications here, Character Plays are very useful projects for any group that intends to progress towards major theatre creation and production. Any group that has created its own Character Play is in an excellent position to understand and to perform good, complex scripted plays. Study of the great Character Plays — by Shakespeare, O'Neill, Kenna, Hewett, Chekhov, etc — becomes clearer and deeper when a Character Playbuilding project has been done beforehand. This is true, of course, for the other types of project described here. In fact, it is generally true to say that people who have been through a positive, successful, creative playbuilding project are better equipped to understand and analyse the creative work of others.

THE SETTING PLAY

Playbuilding around a setting can offer some problems as well as pleasures. The pleasures largely revolve around the variety of life that can be displayed within one setting. Usually, the setting chosen is one steeped in history or mystery and wide open for imaginative drama. The problems are usually those of backbone and dramatic development. It is also easy for a Setting Play to fizzle out to a drab and vague ending.

It is vital to fill the Setting Play with incidents and characters that can of themselves create interest. The setting itself will not hold attention for very long and is of necessity a background. An audience cannot be expected to gaze at the scenery for very long. However, the Setting Play is not so much in need of a plot. It quite thrives on the episodic structure with a variety of activities and people being linked by a single locality. When creating the setting the group should be encouraged to develop the place as one might a character. Don't reveal everything at once; let the secrets of the place come out gradually. Even in the physical presentation there should be hidden and mysterious aspects.

In Darwin I did a play with a group of young writers at a playwrights project. We playbuilt a show called, *The Ghost of Brown's Mart*. Brown's Mart was the name of the theatre we were working in and it had a long history, going back to the days when it was a market and a brothel. This was a one-day project so research was very limited but even so an exciting range of incidents was discovered from the knowledge of local kids and theatre workers on site. In this project we used a lot of lighting and especially sound effects to recreate the historical incidents and conjure up the ghost. The play ended with a chilling 'appearance' by the ghost which was created all round the theatre by the cast using chains and ropes and gentle noises, and the sudden climax of an outside door flung open to flood the theatre with sunlight.

The Setting Play responds well to dramatic poetry — dance, mime, poems, music. It also allows for great contrast of character. Strong contrast of incident will also enrich the Setting Play — love, murder, intrigue and success can all occur in the one place. Attention must be given to filling individual scenes with dramatic tension and to growing suspense which can lead to a satisfactory conclusion for the play.

It would be possible to nominate other categories for types of playbuilt shows, but the basic theatrical elements fit within the four categories I have listed. If a group undertook to create a play in each of these areas they would have an excellent grounding in theatre production and in understanding and analysing any playscript they might be asked to study or perform. As a playbuilding director you may want to create other categories for yourself. Knowing what form of drama is the main driving force for the play is essential to the success of your work. You can use this criterion to refer to, whenever you are in doubt about the suitability of a scene or an idea for the project. Knowing your category well can be as important as having a good, clear title for the play in helping you keep the project driving forward clearly and successfully. You will note that many of the titles of my shows tell you what is going on immediately — *Heroes, Two Nice Kids, Thirteen, Love Matters* — without giving everything away.

All playbuilding projects have certain techniques and problems in common and the next chapters will cover these step by step. It is worth noting that most playbuilding involves the director in trying to achieve many steps at the same time rather than in the neat order to be listed here. The playbuilding process involves the director in being creative, informative, encouraging, open and positive while being critical, honest, analytical and questioning. It's not easy but the rewards are great.

SUMMARY

- Offer and explain options for the play's framework — theme; story; character; setting.
- Theme Play — Episodic play on general topic. Involves large group easily. Encourages varied styles of scene creation. Encompasses all aspects of presentation. Care and precision needed in final structure. Documentary and Compilation plays.
- Story Play — Plot needs to be largely established before scenes are improvised. Develop secondary and parallel plots. Plan carefully and logically. Quest plays.
- Character Play — Caricature and copying. Construct characters with precision. Show characters in interaction. Seek strong structure. Don't let the ending fizzle out.
- Setting Play — Fill setting with rich, diverse life. Use dramatic poetry to evoke atmosphere. Use contrast of character and incident to give dramatic drive. Seek a strong ending.
- Gain group commitment to the general idea of creating a play and performing it, and to the general framework category.
- Gain group commitment to any aspect of the project that has already been decided outside the group.
- Use the framework and the title as your guidelines to test the progress of the work.
- Remain flexible and open to group-suggested variations on the framework.

S.K.Y.

This play was created with an English class of 37 thirteen-year-old boys at Cleveland Boys' High in Sydney. It was done in three weeks of seven forty-minute periods per week. It was an experiment in creative work for the class and no subject restrictions were put on it. The work was difficult at first as the school had a reputation for poor behaviour and low self-esteem. I added to the problems by wasting time on drama exercises. The kids knew the exercises were pointless and reacted accordingly. As the creation of the play developed, so their commitment grew and problems decreased.

A Story Play format was chosen by the group and discussion developed around the idea of passing messages. This seemed appropriate for an English class so I encouraged that line. We began by playing about with the idea of passing the message, 'The sky is falling.' They were familiar with this story and — in days before intense conservation awareness — saw some possible realistic element — in a bit of space-rubbish falling on a kid. They suggested that the play should be about some kids trying to explain this story to adults and the reaction they got. They said quite firmly that no-one would believe them, not because it was a weird story but because they were kids. This element became the theme of the play: no-one listens to kids.

Within the Quest Play framework, we were able to select a range of scenes which were humorous, bizarre or serious. The adult figures were chosen by the boys as examples of the kind of people who would never listen to them. Most of the play was humorous but it was clear where the boys were trying to make a point.

The class were told that they need not be performers as long as they helped create the play. Some had quite small roles but the playbuilding process enabled them all to participate at whatever level they chose. The class insisted on having a Narrator for their story so that it would be fully clear to the audience. This demonstrated that I did not instil enough confidence in their abilities to story tell at the start and was not clear enough about what a Story/Quest Play was and how it could work. A Narrator is not always a bad idea but in this case the role was included to give confidence and so was a rather negative choice. However, my experience has taught me one very valuable lesson — that the director can make numerous mistakes and still steer a group to a successful project as long as he or she remains committed to the group and open to their ideas and creativity.

Much of the play was heavily coloured by the cynical view the boys had of adults. Late in the project when this was clearly revealed by the near-complete play we were able to talk about it. They confirmed that this had been their experience of adults. The play was the first chance they had ever had to say these things in any constructive way.

Many of the dramatic devices arose from sheer enthusiasm. The Cat and the Janitor kept appearing in scenes because these boys wanted to be in the whole play and kept walking into scenes. This was so funny that we decided they should be 'constant motifs' which validated appearances that were silly but had a lovely dramatic logic to them. The Mayor read out a speech about rumours and scare-mongering because the boy playing the role wanted to write the scene. The drawings arose because one boy — a so-called trouble-maker — wanted desperately to draw. He ended up supervising a team of artists. Some of the portrayals were caricatures — the Scientists and Psychiatrists, for example — but others were very real. The Home scene was very unpleasant in its intense verbal violence and the disconnection of all the family members from each other.

A couple of years later I met a boy from this class who had been very enthusiastic and had taken several roles. I asked if he was still doing drama and he said, 'Yeah. But I hate Drama.' I was amazed and said I thought he'd really enjoyed doing our play. He said, 'Yeah, I loved our play, but I hate Drama.' This is an important distinction to remember. The play — the drama — only becomes important to the students if they feel it is theirs. Drama done by numbers can never really belong to the kids; it is just another subject, which some students will resent and reject. Playbuilding can draw deep commitment and intense creativity from all participants and leave them with a feeling of real achievement.

The play, S.K.Y., was performed to other students at the school and to Drama students at the University of New South Wales. It was toured by the Education Department to three other high schools where there was a strong interest in drama. This was a great achievement for the class which was accustomed to its school being looked down upon. In just three weeks, starting with nothing but the suggestion to create a play, these 'ordinary' boys were able to create a play that belonged to them and that was worthy of attention far beyond their expectations.

The teacher reported, in an article for the English Teachers' Association, that comprehension levels in the class rose markedly in later assignments. He also called the project 'one of the most significant events in the educational career of this class'.

Scenario for S.K.Y.

The set was a couple of small tables and a few chairs. The cast stayed in view of the audience at all times. The 'script' used by the cast was simply a list of the scene titles which I have now used in this scenario. Two Heroes were used — Geoff and John. The scenes were linked by a number of different devices. Sometimes the Narrator would introduce the scene; sometimes the scene would begin with obvious dialogue, e.g. picking up an imaginary phone and saying, 'Hello, police station.'; sometimes a drawing was held up to show where the Heroes were or where they were going next.

INTRODUCTION	Narrator sets the scene of two boys sitting in a park.
BEGINNING	Something falls on John's head. It is a piece of the sky, which is invisible. They decide to go to Geoff's Mum who will have it put back.
HOME	Mum and Dad argue over the TV. Geoff tries to tell Mum about the sky. John tells the Cat about it. Mum says to go to their Teacher.
SCHOOL	Teacher tries to keep an unruly class in order. He will not listen to the Heroes and sends them to the Headmaster to be caned for talking. Just as the (real) cane is about to descend, the Narrator interrupts and introduces next scene.
CHURCH	The Priest, with altar boys, takes up the collection. He calls hymn numbers and someone yells, 'Bingo!' They come to the altar to collect the prize. The Heroes try to persuade the Priest to help, but he tells them to pray.
POLICE	The Sergeant tries to deal with calls about a 'streaker', a stolen lawnmower — and a dirty, lazy Constable all at once. The Heroes keep trying to tell him about the sky. Finally the Sergeant decides that the Heroes need psychiatric treatment and sends the dirty Constable for treatment too.
PSYCHIATRISTS	The Psychiatrists are clearly nutty themselves. One spends all his time trying to open an umbrella, and the others keep asking, 'Did you hate your father?' They even ask the Cat. The Janitor comes in, sweeps up and helps the Psychiatrist to open his umbrella.
ADVERTISING	A meeting of the Board of the Magic Glue Company is trying to think of an advertising gimmick. They sing their awful jingle. One suggests they should buy the piece of sky and use it for their ads: 'Magic Glue stuck the sky back.' The Heroes don't trust them and won't sell.
SCIENTISTS	Two Scientists are trying to turn a monkey into a human. A third Scientist walks up and down, shouting, 'Eureka!' and bumping into the wall. The Janitor sweeps up around them all. The Cat plays with the monkey. The Scientists are interested only in their own experiment. As the Heroes leave, the monkey stands up and asks, 'Who were those two nuts?'
TELEVISION INTERVIEW	The famous Newsreader and the Producer are worried because they have no news. The Heroes want them to announce that the sky has to be

patched up. The Producer sends the Interviewer and Cameraman out to ask people what they think of all this. Most of the People wave into the camera and send messages to friends and relatives. The Producer assures the Heroes that he will run the story but a big fire story pushes it off the news.

MAYOR   The Mayor makes a speech to the people warning them against believing the wild rumours the Heroes are spreading.

MAFIA   The Oddfather sends his Boys out to get the Heroes and the piece of sky. The Heroes are about to be shot when the Sergeant and Constables arrive and save them. The whole class becomes either Cops or Mafia, all holding guns on each other. There is a loud bang and everyone falls down dead, except the Heroes.

PRIME MINISTER   The Heroes decide to 'go to the top' to get action. They tell the P.M. their story and that Australia will be doomed if the sky is not fixed. The P.M. makes a political speech about how he will fix everything. The Janitor comes in and sweeps around them all. The Heroes go off, happy that at last there will be action. The P.M. confides in the Cat, 'Cat, I've just had two nuts in here trying to tell me the sky is falling. What do you think of that?'

END   The Narrator returns us to the park where the play began. There are two different boys sitting, talking. Something falls on their heads. It is a piece of the sky.

CHAPTER 2

IDEAS — QUANTITY AND QUALITY

Playbuilding only proceeds when ideas come from the group. While the director must be a creative and contributing figure in the group, little progress can occur if you are the only person putting forward ideas. Your top priority as director, in the first few sessions, is to ensure that a good quantity of ideas comes forward so there is plenty of material to choose from. Your second priority is to gradually improve the quality of the ideas through discussion, questioning, comment and analysis.

Both quantity and quality of ideas will depend very much on an atmosphere of openness and co-operation being established and maintained within the group and between the group and the director. There must be a clear commitment from the director to the project and the group. Playbuilding must never be perceived by young people as some arty game that could end up embarrassing participants in front of their friends and relatives. It has to be a straight-forward, business-like operation that works at creating a strong result.

The group must have confidence that the director will tell them the truth about things, as far as he or she can. Whenever I need to conceal things — to protect a personal confidence or due to the rules of some institution — I tell the group so and give my reason, as honestly as possible. You must establish an atmosphere that tells the group you will be fair at all times and that your decisions will always be based in the needs of the project. This attitude will offer great protection to your group also, because rejection of ideas or criticism of work will always be seen against an objective guide — the needs of the play.

I always come to the early meetings empty-handed; no pen, no paper, no book. Sounds a bit literal but it seems to work. I tell the group that by working together we can create an entertaining, exciting play from nothing. Not a prop, not a costume, not a script in sight, but a fabulous play at the end of it. This attitude also applies to giving drama exercises or games to the group, though I don't do these now. The majority of drama exercises I have seen are designed for actor training and I cannot see any purpose in using them with kids for playbuilding.

Most kids I work with — and certainly most kids in the average classroom — are only interested in drama as a form of creative expression that is useful to them right now. Even at Shopfront Theatre few kids want careers in theatre. This is not surprising. Very few kids who enjoy playing soccer want to go on and play professionally. The more we encourage people to see that theatre is something that can be done successfully as a recreational activity, the more we encourage a real community creativity. The arts should be openly available for everyone to practise, just as sports are.

I occasionally use voice exercises with a group if a play is going to be a huge event and run for some time — for example, when preparing a play for touring. The voice exercises do not actually train the voices in the short period they are used but do make the group aware of vocal needs for theatre and offer some tools for vocal development for the eager few.

Movement exercises can be similarly beneficial. But the need to discipline movement within a performance will arise naturally from the demands made by the play. That discipline will then occur as part of the rehearsal process which will be more effective than from general exercises. A short physical shake-out or loosening up may be useful if your group is a bit lethargic and in many school situations a few minutes of free physical shake-out can be a good way to break away from the usual routine. Do not let this go on too long or the kids will resent the time wasted.

THE REAL START

Once the group is aware of the aims of the project, the types of plays they can choose and the boundaries that need to be laid down, there comes the moment when the director has to ask, 'Any ideas?' This may not be such a difficult moment when there is already a topic or title for the play. That given idea will spark conversation and lots of reaction. Beginning is harder when the group has the whole world to choose from. After asking them to choose something important to them, I also tell them that they must take time over the decision. At this point I used to shut up and just wait, not minding how long a silence we had. And eventually someone would speak up. Nowadays I tend to just chatter on because I find that rambling chatter relaxes most groups more than a tight silence does. As I ramble, I can ask people questions and begin to get some feeling about where the group may like to go with the play. I often tell them about other projects I have done and things other kids were interested in doing. When I spot a topic that seems to interest them I begin to push hard to see if I can get a group commitment. Responses soon let me know if I am on the right track.

I change topics a lot in this early rambling chat, letting my mind and theirs zap about to a whole variety of ideas. When I think I have a topic, I then drop it and try to push another line to see if I can divert them. After a while, I go back to the main topic possibility — sometimes they drag me back to it — to test if they have lost interest or if my guess was right. If it seems to be the right topic for this group, I then press for commitment to the idea. It is not necessary to find the perfect topic because no such thing exists. Almost any topic at all can be turned into a good play. The important thing is to establish that the idea has significance for the group and has been decided upon consciously by the whole group, so that they feel it belongs to them. Dissenters are usually won over within a couple of workshops, as long as they are not a major gang. If they are, and they are still unhappy after a few workshops, the project should not proceed until some general consensus is established.

However, there is little point in pushing a play that the kids clearly don't want to do. At Cleveland Boys' High I once had a class who said they wanted to do a play about children's courts. We work-shopped that for a week of six sessions — with only a three-week period available to us — before I realised that they really did not want to do it. They had chosen the topic because they thought it was a properly serious subject and I had not seen that at the time. When I told them we could now change the topic, everyone wanted to do so. Even though there were now only two weeks left we had no trouble building a good play because the sense of control and freedom delivered to them added real energy and commitment to the project. Also, the early work had developed a group identity and cohesion that gave them the strength to scrap a week's work and choose a theme that really suited them.

The above example supports my earlier point that you should be careful when demanding commitment, that you do not insist on a decision before the group is ready. In most continuing groups

Final song from *Childmyth*. Original cast.

the commitment grows gradually and you ask for small commitments constantly, building up an overall dedication to the work. But when problems are occurring in a project and the work does not flow, very often the fault lies in lack of commitment. This can occur because the group does not have enough confidence in themselves or in the idea of playbuilding. Often it is because the group dynamics or the group history make commitment a difficult action for them. You may have to seize an appropriate moment and demand commitment — or stop.

Naturally, the director will be disappointed if a project stops but the options have to be put fairly to the group and not in terms of punishment. Demanding a commitment — in very clear terms — enables you and the group to solidify rapidly the achievements to date and to begin afresh. But it should only be made a major issue if it is clear the work is going badly astray and the demand must not be made too early, before the group have discovered what it really is they are embarked upon.

FLOW OF IDEAS

Once a topic/idea is agreed upon, the floodgates of ideas open. The director must establish with the group the basic attitudes as to which ideas are most useful and how decision-making will occur. You must make it clear that there are no right answers, or answers hidden in your head that you want them to ferret out. As you establish that what you really want, and what the project really needs, is creative ideas from their own heads and their own experience, you should also make it clear that you will accept almost anything put forward and, with group discussion, decide if the ideas fit the needs of the play — not if they are 'good' or 'bad' ideas, but if they fit this particular play. You should adopt a non-judgemental stance; see everything as grist to the mill of the play. Sometimes early in the piece kids will try to test you by trying to shock you with naughty ideas but that soon disappears. Sometimes I find that I might have to discuss racism or sexism with a group to prevent them from, inadvertently, promoting such ideas. This can be done quite simply by pointing out how and why an audience would regard an idea as, say, racist. I then ask if they want to put a racist scene in their play. The answer is invariably no and the next question is to find out how to use positive parts of the idea or to fix up the scene that may be racist.

This type of discussion occurs often, and about all sorts of issues of logic and intent. The director must challenge every idea and scene where intention and result seem to be at odds. You should present the problems from the point of view of an enlightened audience member. And the question, 'How would an audience react to this?' should be asked often. This is especially important with comedy. Quite often the jokes and humour that a group devises can be rather 'in' for the group and so hilarious to them. But it may be dull and meaningless to an audience. Going back to the idea of audience reaction is also a protective device for the group and a way to keep reminding them that, no matter how much fun playbuilding is, the project is work and work with a definite purpose. The protection is there for you and the group because you can discuss ideas fairly objectively with them by using audience reaction as guide.

Second-hand ideas should be discouraged at early stages of the project and you must put emphasis on originality and personal experience. Of course, later, you will probably want to encourage the borrowing of material from other sources, especially from literature and pop-culture, to bring a further dimension to the work. But early emphasis should be on making a play that belongs to this group. Once the group's creativity is securely established, borrowing becomes informed selection of found material. A piece borrowed from Shakespeare or from a pop-song becomes a reference point chosen for its appropriateness, rather than a way to evade creating something for themselves, as it can be in early sessions.

During these early sessions the decision-making process will become clear. The group will learn that the director is quite happy to let them make all the decisions as long as there is discussion and reasonable agreement. The director will appear as someone who can offer trustworthy information — even expertise — on theatrical and dramatic methods; and who asks lots of hard questions but provides few answers. The director will insist on clarity and quality in the processing of ideas — just as he or she will later insist on clarity and quality in the presentation of the final play. The director will always praise good work and always encourage, but won't cheat about standards.

Playbuilding can only progress successfully if the director establishes high standards in all aspects of the work. Every member of the group must know that they will only be told their work is good when it reaches a truly worthy standard, but that they will be encouraged every step of the way towards that standard. That worthy standard should be one that is within the range that you believe the group can reach, but probably slightly beyond what they themselves expect to reach.

PLAYBUILDING TO A SET TOPIC OR TITLE

It is far preferable for a first-time group to have free choice of a topic. This enables them to experience the excitement of their own creativity bound only by their own rules — the need to create the play — and also to experience you as an open, creative director who is very much on their side in this drama adventure. A first 'free' project will also develop a sense of confidence in the group's own abilities to create. If a successful playbuilding project, based in free choice, is achieved then in later projects any problems associated with setting a topic for the group become easy to deal with. They will already know that they will have a big creative input to any playbuilding project and it is easy to reassure them that even with a set topic this will be so.

It is necessary as director to work hard to keep enthusiasm high for a set project. You must sell it to the group sometimes. Within a school system, setting a playbuilding topic can sometimes generate an automatic response of rejection or lethargy. The strongest point in your favour is that studying any topic through playbuilding is almost always more exciting than any other way of handling it.

You will find that even the most rigid of topics will still allow room for the group to make quite a few decisions about the emphasis of the material and the style and direction the play will take. Allow the group to make these decisions right at the start so that they feel that sense of control and ownership. Encourage innovative approaches to the topic; encourage early selection of a title; encourage lots of humour so that they do not think the project will be dry and dull. Use lots of your most lateral and tangential thinking to demonstrate that the approach to a set topic does not have to be predictable. Keep challenging their ingenuity. All these suggestions apply to all playbuilding but are essential for work on the set topic.

THE QUIET, THE LOUD AND THE UGLY

Once formalities are over, ideas usually come in bombardment. The early workshop sessions are often fairly chaotic with lots of talking over the top of each other, lots of verbal shoving, minds racing with clever snatches of thought and image. Out of all this melee the group will rely on you to select the ideas most appropriate and most useful for the play. You must take care that the flow is not discouraged but at the same time be rigorous in the testing of ideas.

The Uglies have two ways of manifesting themselves. They will suggest silly things — to draw attention to themselves or out of fear that their real ideas might be rejected. That's easy because they and everyone else know that the suggestions are not serious. This makes it easy to wave them aside; no point being aggressive because that can so easily stop any steps towards serious participation. A nice trick is to take, occasionally, one of these silly ideas quite seriously and show the group that it could work. This has the effect of letting the group know how surprising and flexible drama can be. It often shakes the Uglies out of their silliness too.

The other ploy of the Uglies is to laugh at the ideas of the others and try to make other kids seem ridiculous, especially those who commit themselves early and strongly to the work. As everyone will be rather sensitive about tossing their thoughts and experiences about, it is important that such demoralising comments be taken up and banished. I find myself often spending time in early workshops proving that 'unworkable' ideas can actually be made to work. This can be difficult as you finally have to reject most of these ideas. I usually call upon other plays I have done where a similar idea cropped up and was used, but point out it is not appropriate to our present play. Your knowledge of theatre and play texts will also come to the fore in these cases. Someone who is being put down can be quite thrilled to hear that this idea was used by Shakespeare in some play. One secret I have discovered is that, while kids profess to hate or not understand Shakespeare, they also know he was the greatest so that any comparison with him is taken as the ultimate drama compliment.

It is important that you do not allow put-downs to go unchallenged. If they are made to feel foolish at any time they will clam up and enough of that can kill the play. Even if your explanation of how an idea could be made to work is a bit shaky, the group and the kid concerned will still see that you are taking every possibility seriously and are prepared to defend them. And — sometimes — that weird idea that seems out of place and a bit foolish can turn out to be a new perspective.

If possible, say yes to every idea immediately. That will give confidence and energy to the group. An idea can always be rejected after it has been tried out in improvisation and it can always be edited out of the play later if it isn't working. If there is not enough time to try every idea through improvisation — almost always the case — you and the group must list all the ideas and then decide together which will be tried. No idea should ever be rejected because some certain person put it forward. Ideas must always be accepted or rejected on their merits. Any other practice will undermine the quality of the playbuilding.

The Loud are probably irritating but their volume is a sign of their enthusiasm. The Loud should be constantly challenged to provide substance and greater complexity. The Loud can be very useful because they will save you from lack of volunteers when you start to improvise the scenes. They are happy to lead the way and it is then easier for you to draw others in. There is nothing wrong with the Loud being given major roles and a larger share of the work. In playbuilding everyone works to their own level of energy and confidence and I see no value in forcing an introverted kid to take a leading role. Encourage, urge, give every opportunity, yes, but finally each individual must decide what commitment they will make. I rather like the Loud as long as their real contribution is equal to their volume. They can often be a great help to you also in leading a group to higher levels of performance.

The Quiet can also be rather special contributors to a group. I fully empathise with painful shyness or lack of confidence and I insist that no-one must ever be compelled to perform in a play. A playbuilding project can offer many jobs to shy people who do not want to go on stage — creating the play itself; recording of the play; music; lights; sound; stage-management; design; etc. However, in my experience, it is very rare for a participant in a playbuilding project to decide not to be in the play.

It is often from the Quiet that the most penetrating ideas come; maybe because they are thinking more and talking less. You must listen carefully for the whispered comment, the soft aside, the tentative suggestion. All these are being drowned out by the fifty other shouted or argued ideas that happen simultaneously. Pick up the comments of the Quiet as well and bring them to the fore when they are deserving of group attention.

PROTECTING THE GROUP

As director you have to provide a lot of protection for your group all through the process and presentation. The need to protect begins early. I have mentioned the need to protect kids from ridicule and to protect the quiet ones from being lost in the noise. There is also the protection of not demanding feats that are risky or beyond their abilities and of vetoing foolhardy suggestions. One early rule I also impose: no-one is allowed to volunteer anyone else. This veto includes the director who can encourage involvement but not order it. It prevents kids from trying to embarrass each other, but still permits them to give out information that Sue is a great juggler or Bill plays piano, etc. This rule also protects people who feel unsure about what may be demanded of them. They learn from the start that they will not be made to do anything they don't choose to do.

The other essential protection is emotional. In the rush and excitement of creating a play, some people find themselves revealing more about their lives, families and dreams than they normally would. That can sometimes be embarrassing or even painful. The creative process encourages people to open up and to trust the group and the project. As director you must ensure that all revelations are treated as ideas for a play so that comment and discussion can be objective. This eases pressure on anyone who has revealed something too personal. It often helps to add and subtract characters and incidents to convert revelations into fiction.

I always give the person who suggests a major scene the opportunity to direct it or perform in it so that they can shape it away from or towards being a revelation. Some people want a scene to be realistic as a way of understanding the real event and they should be allowed that choice, but not be treated as people who are going through therapy. How individual creators use the work for their internal needs is up to them. The director must protect the group from amateur psychologising by dealing with each incident as material for creating theatre.

This fixed viewpoint enables the most powerful and exciting learning, healing and growth to occur. Positive growth is the natural result of creative activity. It is easy to let people know publicly that you have noticed their positive actions and work and to praise them without taking away the inner privacy that many young people need when creating and growing. Public praise should happen often in playbuilding but invasions of privacy should never happen.

Your observations or theories about emotional development should be kept to yourself in workshops and shared in confidence with colleagues who understand the processes of creative work. It is always gratifying to see emotional development, especially when parents notice as well and thank you for bringing about positive transformations in their kids. They will also blame you, of course, if the kids become 'too independent'. Just remember that the effects arise naturally from creative work and that you do your part best by providing a safe, working environment. As a responsible adult working with kids you would, of course, take appropriate action in cases of real danger and abuse to young people that came to your knowledge through the work.

In a play on the theme of prejudice, we had made very rapid progress and the small group was honest and forthcoming with their experiences. In our fourth session a girl raised the issue of prejudice against sick people. She set up a scene in which a girl reveals she has a terminal illness and is then rejected by her friend and later by her boyfriend. In discussion of the scene the girl told us that she had been diagnosed as suffering from a form of leukemia. She said that it was very important to her to include her scene in our play — which was due for a one-off, open day presentation just two weeks later. Despite the fact that some members of the group seemed worried by this idea, I agreed. It seemed clear to me that if this group, to whom she had offered this harrowing experience, were to reject her scene we would be compounding the rejections she had received.

The next week some of the group came to me and said they felt it would be unfair for the scene to be presented publicly as it was too personal and would upset the girl's family. I explained to them how vital it was that we did not appear to reject the girl. I also told them I didn't believe for one minute that the girl would allow the scene to go into the performance, but workshopping it and being given permission to decide for herself about using it were clearly important responsibilities that she wanted to have. I later talked to the girl, privately and told her the others were worried for her and her family. She said that she had been thinking about it and wanted to leave the scene out of the performance so that she did not hurt other people. The situation could have become unpleasant for everyone, but by our keeping faith with the boundaries and objective rules of playbuilding, even in this very stressful circumstance, this girl had the chance to use the workshop in the way she needed without disrupting the work of the group. The poignancy of this girl's need to work through her experience by using playbuilding added an urgency and edge to the work of all of us. The play gained daring and strength from that unpresented scene.

If the girl had been too emotionally entangled to decide to omit the scene I would have found reasons for the omission. The major reason would have been the stress to the group of performing such an upsetting scene effectively for an audience, knowing it was true. Revealing that fact had transformed the scene into something much more than, and very different from, theatre. Such a verdict would not have involved rejection or criticism of the content of the scene itself, simply a decision on its use in the play.

PROTECTING THE GROUP FROM YOURSELF

Take steps to protect the group from yourself; your ego can destroy a project if it becomes rampant. While the director has to be an active, creative part of the group, he or she must also be careful not to swamp the project and the group with adult knowledge of the world and adult sensibilities. Your values must not be used as a touchstone. Every value, every idea, every attitude must be up for examination. Remember that the play belongs to the kids, not to you. There is nothing more refreshing than hearing genuine opinions of the young in a play — there is nothing more stale and dreary than watching a group of young people mouth the opinions of their elders in some sad attempt to please. Your job is to question every opinion put forward until the group is satisfied about what it wants to say. You need not agree with what the group says; but you have to be satisfied that you have made them test and re-test their ideas and that nothing is being presented without thought and analysis. When the play is ready to be shown, it must be theirs. You will be erased from the project.

The more it appears that you had nothing to do with the play, the better you did your job. That can be a bit of a letdown but it is a necessary part of a really good playbuilding process.

The final success of a performance of a playbuilt show depends not on the quality of the performances, not on the quality of the theatrical devices, not even on the quality of the play's structure, which is so important, but almost entirely on the quality of the thinking that has gone into the devising of the play. If the quality of thought and analysis and questioning is high enough, then all else will follow and many other shortcomings can be overlooked.

An example of adult domination and near ruination of a good idea happened when I was directing a play for an overseas festival we had been invited to. The play was on the theme of peace — (*Piece by Piece*, see Chapter Eleven) — and a colleague was sitting in on the project. We had talked about war a lot and the question had been raised about whether the kids in the group could imagine themselves killing someone and if so, in what situation that might be, apart from a war. My colleague immediately broke in and declared that this was a silly idea because no-one in that room would ever be capable of killing anyone; life was sacred; we weren't that sort of people. By the time she had finished, none of the kids could have said they could imagine killing without making themselves sound like total barbarians. She had imposed a moral blackout on their thinking.

Knowing this woman fairly well, I asked, 'What would you do if you had a gun and you saw someone cutting the ears off a live kitten with a pair of scissors?' She replied angrily, 'Well, someone like that doesn't deserve to live!' She had the good grace to laugh at being caught out. The discussion then proceeded more openly. Most of the group claimed that there were certain conditions under which they could imagine killing.

After a lot of discussion we created a very effective scene which used as its format the shape of my original question about the kitten. In the play's Sydney performances the scene was powerful but not exactly what we wanted. In discussion with audience members it was pointed out that the scene could be viewed as politically unbalanced and therefore unfair. Every speaker at the end of their speech referred back to the power of the President of the U.S.A. to press a button and wipe out the world with a nuclear war. Other people, of course, have this same power so the scene appeared anti-American. We then changed the scene to include all the admitted nuclear nations. This irony — that though most humans might be prepared to kill for personal reasons, none would ever drop a nuclear bomb — and the added list of nuclear nations made the scene absolutely frightening. That extra ounce of precision in the thought behind the scene added a pound of power to the performance.

When I spoke to my colleague about the workshop, she saw my point about leaving the discussion as open and value-free as possible but insisted that there had to be some absolutes. For example, she said, we could not say that destruction of the human race was no bad thing. Well, I won't even agree with that in a playbuilding discussion, because it might just be a better thing for the universe to lose humans; something better than us might evolve once we're gone. In a world where most values are under question from some direction; where home and family concepts are tainted by child-abuse statistics; where school and church are frequently reviled; where the law attracts contempt; where drug-culture often dominates reality; where violence invades streets, transport, homes and sport; and where kids see all this every day on TV and can see many good reasons to lose faith in adult institutions, it is hard to hold firm values let alone absolute ones. The process of playbuilding can enable kids to decide for themselves what they want to say about their world and what questions they want to ask. Learning how to think with precision and clarity and how to ask good questions can be a very useful weapon and/or shield in this modern world.

THINK POSITIVE!

It seems to be true that drama thrives on conflict, problems and the negative in life. Who wants to see a play in which everyone romps about smelling flowers and saying how great life is while nothing really happens except that the sun comes out and everyone is happy? So why should we expect that young people when they become playbuilders (which is just another word for the real meaning of 'playwrights') will fill their stage worlds with positive people and relate glowing tales of happiness for all? This is just another manifestation of the adult desire that 'children shouldn't grow up too soon'; that one day a child's potential will be realised and he or she will suddenly be an adult.

Playbuilding must accept young people for what they are right now, right at the time they are creating this play. That means accepting that they are real people living with the real problems of a real world. In fact, their lives have more than sufficient strife and misunderstanding round and about them for any drama.

The issues that groups express through their plays will often involve a 'negative view' of life. That's fine. I believe that kids should be allowed to voice their concern about the arms race; the destruction of the earth's environment; the starvation in the world; violence of all kinds; physical and mental abuse of children; racism and sexism; the destructive elements of families and schooling; and any other examples of unfairness in the world, to which kids seem to be so sensitive. But it is also the director's role to push for the positive, to push for hope.

Your 'positive' role as director is not to insist on avoiding bleak subjects but to insist on examining all aspects of them. Plays cannot be expected to provide answers to all the questions they raise — but they can offer a tone of optimism. Merely by raising an issue and by creating a play, a group is taking positive action. The natural humour that young people seem to bring to all their work is another highly positive aspect of their plays. Encourage the humour and suggest that even the bleakest issue can be aired in a way that still leaves the audience with hope. But don't insist that they put a rainbow in at the end of every play.

Childmyth (at the end of this chapter) begins by examining all the usual unpleasant issues of how young people are treated and mistreated in our society. But a point came when we all decided that we would try to suggest something more 'rainbowish' about youth and the lives of young people. We did this by stressing the obvious pleasures and virtues of being young — hope, strength, love, joy, innocence, dreams. We also embarked on an exciting idea to create 'new myths' and we did this mostly through chants, movement and symbolism. I have to confess that the final song in *Childmyth* is rather a rainbow song, but the strong chants of renewing and changing the world that preceded the song did build an acceptable atmosphere for such sunshine. And audiences tended to leave with broad smiles on their faces, which cannot be entirely a bad thing.

SUMMARY

Ideas
- Establish open, non-judgemental atmosphere to draw barrage of ideas.
- Discuss, question, analyse ideas to sharpen quality. Banish borrowed ideas in early sessions.
- Choose ideas as a group and according to the objective needs of the play.
- Although a brief physical shake-out may be useful, drama exercises and games are unnecessary and even detrimental.
- Push for commitment when you sense a group feeling for some topic.
- There are no 'right' answers in the early work. Later, correctness is decided objectively according to the rules or boundaries established by ongoing group decisions.
- Challenge scenes where intention and results seem at odds.
- Set high but reachable standards.
- Give praise publicly and fully but only when you mean it and it is deserved.

With a set topic
- Explain fully why topic was chosen, then work really hard to draw commitment.
- Let the group make early decisions on style, emphasis and title.

Quiet, Loud, Ugly
- Do not allow put-downs to go unchallenged.
- Insist on substance as well as volume from the Loud.
- Listen carefully for Quiet contributions.

Protecting the group
- Protect individuals from ridicule and from being submerged by the group.
- Do not encourage physical risks.
- No-one must volunteer anyone else. The director can encourage, but never order.
- All scenes are part of the play — even personal revelations — and are assessed as such.
- Don't practise amateur psychology on the kids.
- Don't swamp them with your adult knowledge, values and sensibilities. It is their play, not yours!
- *Think positive* — Do not avoid bleak subjects but examine all aspects of them. Drama thrives on conflict and problems, but do push for hope.
- Quality of thought is all! Question and challenge constantly.

CHILDMYTH

Childmyth was created at Shopfront as a special project for the International Year of the Child. I created the title and gathered a group of ten young people — five boys and five girls, aged from twelve to sixteen — to work on devising the play. The title and the Year suggested the themes. The play was created over about twenty workshops and some scenes involved other young people at Shopfront in their creation. We also did an early presentation of work-in-progress and the ensuing long discussions with the audience — mostly parents — helped in further development of the play. We wanted the play to be a celebration of being young, without avoiding some of its difficulties.

The play combined material from history and mythology with scenes about the lives of the performers, original songs and an attempt at creating 'new myths'. The play was very successful and had an extended season at Shopfront. It also performed at a Youth Forum. The next year it was revived as a Theatre-in-Education play with a cast of seven — only one of whom had been in the original cast — and toured to schools, performing to more than ten thousand students. The ABC made a television program about the group — called the Shopfront Caravan — and scenes from *Childmyth* were central to the program which was shown nationally. A script of the T.I.E. version of the play was written up for the TV show and was published by Shopfront.

Scenario for CHILDMYTH

Theatre-in-Education production by Shopfront Theatre; directed by E. B. Cast: Martin Blacker; Nick Carlile; Peta Carlile; Brian McCarty; Fiona Robertson; Liane Robinson; Gerry Tacovsky.

This is the scenario for the touring production with a cast of seven. A script was written for the touring version because it was needed for a television show made about the group. At Shopfront the play was performed on a carpet-square with a few chairs at the back, the Childmyth box — a solid, trunk-like box that was placed on its side or on end to provide different levels — and the props. The cast remained on stage all through the show. Each cast member had an individual costume but all were simple clothes, except for the Clown character who wore a bright, striped outfit and a Jester's cap. The Clown carried a magic staff which had a small doll, dressed in his image, on top. The main feature of the design was the use of large coloured cloths. Some were plain, sheet-like cloths, dyed in pastel colours. There was a special gold and white cloth used for the creation of gods and kings; and a heavy cloth with the word *Childmyth* sewn on to it, patchwork style. This was used as a catching net at the end of the play and was laid out at the start with all the props on it. The major prop was a large sun mask in gold, trimmed in red, with a suggested face on it, which was held by two performers. Other masks were worn by the cast in later scenes.

There were a number of songs in the show, all written by me with music by Martin Blacker. The songs were based on workshop discussions with the original cast.

SETTING	The play begins with the stage all set up. The Childmyth box is on its side at the Front. The Childmyth cloth is laid out flat with a number of props on it. Stage Left, three boys stand covered by the plain coloured cloths.
	(Note: In the original production the three boys were blond look-alikes who suggested different stages of youth. In this version we emphasised the types of characters — child, student, lover.)
	The rest of the cast are at the back.
'ALL THE WORLD'S . . .'	As Peta and Liane, in unison, say a version of the Shakespeare speech, they unveil the boys, each in a pose suitable to his character. In a version of the 'O, for a Muse of fire' speech, they say that this stage will hold the history of childhood.
NURSERY RHYMES	Versions of nursery rhyme jokes and other poems. Jack and Jill. Old lady

and the shoe. 'Infant Sorrow' by Blake. Mary and her little lamb. 'Somewhere over the rainbow' is interrupted by 'Follow the yellow brick road', to which everyone dances.

ALICE
Some end up around the Childmyth box as the tea-party from *Alice in Wonderland*, using simple props including Mickey Mouse ears for the Dormouse. The Clown recites some of 'The time has come' and the rest act out the 'say what you mean' bit of the tea-party.

PRINCE CHARMING
Martin, in plastic tiara, says he is Prince Charming. He holds up a thong that his partner lost at the ball. The girls clamour for it but Nick recognises it as his.

SNOW WHITE
They march about on their knees in little caps, singing, 'Hi ho, hi ho, it's off to work we go.' Snow White is busy working. Dwarfs all sing and giggle. She hates their stupid song and is fed up with slaving for them. 'I think I'll go and eat a poisoned apple.'

PIED PIPER
Brian, the Clown, plays pipe that draws kids to him. Parent asks, 'What is this music that draws our children?' It turns into the Mickey Mouse Club song as the kids dance off. After the kids go, the Parent says, 'Now I can do all the things I've always wanted to do.'

SONG
'When I Grow Up' — Each performer has a verse and each verse has a little twist. Nick wants to be a nurse because a nurse is a caring thing to be. Fiona wants to be a secretary — Secretary-General of the United Nations. Gerry wants to be an astronaut, or a waiter. Peta wants to be a dancer because she is a dancer now. Martin wants to be a garbage-man because you find lots of great things in garbage and without garbage-men we'd be knee-deep in it. Brian wants to be a spy because he likes dressing up in disguises. They all sing that they hope their generation grow up to be cowards so that everyone will run away from wars. They hope their friends will grow up to be children and retain joy and hope. They hope adults will grow down and find the positive things of childhood again.

MODELS FOR KIDS — PARENTS
This is announced. Mum and Dad are bombarded with demands by their children. The Parents point out that now they have grown up and they have to be doctor, chauffeur, dietician, social worker, etc, etc. Most of all they have to be models — don't smoke, don't drink. All is for the good of the children.

MODELS FOR KIDS — TEACHERS
Personal reminiscences about teachers; some good, some bad. These are interspersed with schoolyard chants, finishing with, 'Build a bonfire, build a bonfire, Put the teachers on the top, Put the prefects in the middle, And burn the bloody lot.'

MODELS FOR KIDS — POP STARS
Three different versions of a simple song by three 'stars' of different eras. The last, most disgusting star is mobbed.

MODELS FOR KIDS — TV
One-liners about the TV of the day. The soapie segment has dialogue like: 'And I'll be the lesbian.' 'You're always the lesbian. It's our turn.' 'If I can't be the lesbian, I'm not gonna play.' They finish the scene by realising it is four o'clock and time for children's TV. They all sit in front of an imaginary TV set and hold a TV-watching pose for a long time.

(Note: To this point the play had been extremely energetic and raced along at a cracking pace. The TV 'slump' got lots of laughs and was a complete change of pace that linked effectively into the next scene. The scenes up to this point were also full to the brim of childhood references. This provided a rich mixture of quick impressions that drew the audience in strongly as all the material was familiar and was presented in humorous style. The shape of the play was structured in this way, to draw audiences from the familiar into more and more unusual ideas.)

THE HISTORY OF CHILDHOOD
Stories are acted out as each Narrator tells a brief history. Children as sacrifices to the gods. The Children's Crusade. Legends of parents eating their children.

MARTIN'S LOVE SONG
'No-one's ever loved me although I am now sixteen'. Martin sings a little of the song and then interrupts it with a funny story about being in love with his teacher and with a girl when he was fourteen, but . . . 'I mean who wants a pudgy fourteen-year-old with braces, glasses and a bad case of oozing pimples?'

'THE STEREOTYPE SHOW'
Song with monologues. The boys sing about being the stereotype show because they all have to fit into a 'model'. Gerry is quiet and mysterious — 'I'm quiet 'cause I've nothing to say.' Brian is vague and a 'druggie'. Nick is sexy and walks on girls who throw themselves at his feet — 'They shouldn't have been lying there in the first place.' Martin is the musician, who doesn't care about image.

'SIXTEEN AND A GIRL'
Sung by Liane and Fiona.
'When you're sixteen and you happen to be a girl,
Life can be sad.
When you find your body is something to cover up,
Except to flaunt at the beach.
When modesty is female and lust is masculine,
And teenage boys are scared of sex.'

The song goes on from there to examine other contradictions in popular attitudes to girls and their sexuality, including that masturbation 'belongs to boys' — the most provocative idea in the play for many people. The song ends rather gently and romantically.

(Note: This song was subject to several re-writes and close analysis, especially by the girls. It was in these discussions about issues involving the roles of the girls in this play as well as in our society that a lot of the new and interesting work of the play evolved. The 'new myths' of the play — following — arose directly from this work which involved most of the kids of Shopfront in the workshopping. It was interesting that in the rehearsals for the first production, i.e. after the structure had been set, some of the boys asked if we could leave out 'The Stereotype Show' because they didn't like it — not because it was not accurate. The girls pointed out to them the significance of their request.)

THE AFFIRMATION OF THE FEMININE
Peta begins a chant that the other girls pick up in rounds. 'I'm a girl. I'm a girl. I'm a flower. I'm a girl. Reach the sun. I'm a girl. I'm the moon. I'm a girl. The feminine is in me.' Music plays behind the chant which becomes very powerful. The boys pick up some of the central statements. 'I'm the moon. The feminine is in me.' The boys adopt 'passive' positions; two hug while one sits with a doll. Martin is playing the music. The girls push the chant strongly.

SONG FOR GIRLS
'Girls were born to be equal in all the things they choose to do, Girls aren't pink and boys aren't blue'. The song goes on to press the case for women to be respected as full human beings. They do not want to compete with men but teach them to co-operate. The song finishes with the girls proclaiming that soon they'll be women, 'And when we are we'll change the world.'

(Note: Although the play was done at a time when women's issues were very topical, some adults were a bit shocked by hearing girls talk about their sexuality and by the strength of the stance taken by the girls. Putting many of the views into song form helped make them more acceptable. School audiences reacted positively to the play and teachers were pleased to see the issues raised. The boys got little flak about their 'gentle' moments in the play.)

'HAMLET' A brief but strong encounter, with sexual undertones, between Hamlet and his mother.

THE DOLL Fiona plays with her doll, dressing it and speaking to it. As she does, Liane has her face painted in bright, doll-like patterns and is moved about like a doll. As Fiona talks baby-talk to the doll, Liane intersperses live-doll statements — 'My grandma thinks I'm beautiful'; 'The man next door gives me a toffee every time I kiss him'; 'I think boys are silly'; etc. Finally Liane goes to the doll and tells it how alike they are but she is determined to grow up and be all the aspects of herself that she likes.

SONG — 'BURN' Adults say 'don't' all the time but the kids are burning to dare and learn and grow. 'But I'll burn and burn and burn. I'll never be just a glow, I'll always be a flame, No matter how old I grow'.

NEW MYTH This scene uses a lot of visual elements, all happening together and then picks up many strands from the earlier myth and history sections of the play to develop a pattern leading towards an image of re-birth and an image of sacrifice.

Nick twirls long ribbons on a stick about the stage. The coloured cloths are billowed high into the air and brought billowing down, like parachutes. Liane keeps reaching for the cloths but they are billowed out of her reach. She plays 'Burn' on a whistle. The others gradually wrap the cloths about her, moving as if around a maypole. They unwrap her and then lie her on the floor as if dead. The sheets are billowed over her and allowed to cover her. Gerry places a mask on the 'body' — 'What is it to die but to stand naked in the wind and melt into the sun?' They peel the cloths off Liane and raise her and embrace her. Nick announces, 'Childmyth'.

CHILDMYTH As a series of myths are mentioned, the cast put on masks, made from their own faces. Cain and Abel. Cronus and Zeus eating their children. Narcissus. The sacrifice of Ipheginia. Orestes and Electra. Abraham ready to kill his son. Herod slaying the children. Nick stands on the box and tries to fly to the sun. He falls back into Peta's arms and dies. They sing two verses of 'Burn' very softly over his body. They each repeat a line from the play as they take off their masks and place them about the stage. 'Am I my brother's keeper?' 'I will fly and fly to the sun'. 'The affirmation of the feminine.' The box is upended and Liane is lifted on top as a strong chant is built up. 'The ritual of blood, ceremony of blood, child blood, child ceremony, ritual of child blood'. The Childmyth cloth is brought to the front of the box and they billow it up and down as they chant. 'We'll change the world, renew the world, relive the world.' Liane calls 'Childmyth!' and leaps from the box into the cloth.

(Note: In the original production a boy — much smaller than Liane — was lifted from the floor and flung high into the air and then caught in the cloth. The moment in both productions looked quite daring.)

SONG *Childmyth* Rousing finale of positive statements about youth. 'We've got the song, we'll share it with you.' The last shouted word of the song was, 'Childmyth!'

CHAPTER 3

IMPROVISATION DEVELOPING AND REFINING IDEAS

The main tool in playbuilding for forging ideas into drama is improvisation. This is a wonderfully flexible process that requires no special equipment or space or preparation to work successfully. A big room is always nice but not essential. I find it hard to get good improvisations going outdoors — too many distractions — but it can be done anywhere really. It can be done with a minimum of words and/or a minimum of action. But it should be done in the early sessions with a maximum of group involvement. This means that even if there are only two kids needed to work the scene all the others should watch and then be involved in the discussion and enrichment process that leads to the impro being done again so that it develops. I only split a class or group into smaller segments for impros if I am doing a one-off workshop or demonstration, or if I have a very experienced group. Splitting the group early also splits the commitment and can lead to destructive ideas of competition.

Any time I do split the group into smaller segments and ask them to develop scenes, I make sure I visit each group in turn so they have someone to talk to and bounce ideas off as they build their scene. Each scene is shown to the whole group and then there is discussion so that the whole group can be involved in analysing and developing the scene. The whole group then has a vested interest in every scene.

Once the discussion gets underway in a workshop it can be tempting to talk on too much. Watch to see when the kids have made their commitment to the project and then get some of them on their feet, doing a scene. This will show them early in the project that turning the ideas into bits of drama and bits of performance is quite easy. I am something of a talker and I quite like getting a really solid discussion base to every project. But I do try to ensure that at least one scene is created in the first session, even if we have not yet decided on the topic. I try to select a fairly simple scene idea so that there will be room for the group to edit and expand on the work. If the group's first impro is set up in too complex a way it may fail and make future work very difficult. If no topic has been decided upon I use some idea that has been talked about in the session for a starting point and tell the group we need to do it so they can see how we can turn ideas into scenes.

I rarely use words to the group like 'improvise' and never ask them to 'act'. I try to be vague in these early sessions about the process so that they can bring their own style to it. I never, ever show them how to improvise; the very words forbid it. I use terms like 'Show me.' My side of the conversation would go something like this: 'Okay, so we'll do the family thing that Bill described. The one with the broken-down car. Can you show us that, Bill? Get some people. How many do you need? Who wants to do this? Anyone want to be Dad? Do you want to do this, Bill, or will you just tell them what happens?' By this time, with a group new to playbuilding, a bit of an improvisation will be happening. Do not let them start until Bill or the group has given enough information to sustain a fair amount of work, but ensure it is not too complicated yet.

After the first impro begins I let it run and drift until it really does grind to a halt or until the group bring it to a dramatic conclusion. You must not keep interrupting improvisations, especially the early ones. It is very tempting to do so because you see them struggling and getting nowhere and you think you know just what they should say or do. But they must start to develop their own impro abilities and that will never happen unless they are allowed time on their feet to manage the material. It does not matter if most of the material they create is not usable, even boring. All you and the group need is material to work on. If you distil a few good seconds out of a long impro then you have a base to build further on. The impro is not finished when its performers stop because that is when the whole group become playwrights in the full sense of the word and start fashioning the material into drama.

Another big advantage of allowing impros to drift is that very often the performers will come up with their best and most dramatic solutions and inventions when they are stretched to that point of real dramatic need: when the whole thing becomes so boring that only a fresh jolt of dramatic energy can revive it. If they do not meet that need the scene comes to a halt anyway, so nothing is lost. But there is a great deal to be gained by allowing the scene to ramble, bog down, lose its way, drift, change its point of view, stall, re-start, etc. Let all those things happen to the performers and give them the opportunity to think and work their way out of it on their feet. If no solutions appear, you take it back to the group and discuss, suggest, invent a way to a better scene which can then be tried out for further appraisal and change. Most scenes will continue changing through successive workshops until you reach the point where the process becomes a rehearsal rather than play-creation.

In the early stages of impros I do not bother much about the performers sustaining concentration and characterisations and 'reality'. If they giggle in the middle of creating a scene, I don't mind. If they stop and ask questions of the group or of me, I let that happen. Naturally, I demand more and more concentration and discipline as we develop the play. This is another vital part of the playbuilding process to remember: it is a *process*. Do not expect all the difficult things to be achieved at once. Do not put unnecessary pressure on the group, especially at the beginning. The first steps into creating their own play are difficult to take. It can be embarrassing; it can be daunting; it can make a kid feel inadequate. We are asking them to do something that is easy if taken in small steps but which is an amazing task if you look ahead to the end-product.

Remember that they are standing there in front of a group of their peers and a director/teacher figure, showing what happened to them on some occasion or what they imagine an event would be. They're not sure how to make it 'dramatic'. They're not sure how much of the story to tell. They're not sure if the way they are doing it is satisfactory. And they certainly are not sure yet how doing this little scene is going to lead everybody to a play that will actually be performed for people and entertain them. In the light of all this uncertainty and struggle, telling someone not to giggle or that they must concentrate will only detract from the hard job they are trying to do. After all, you did not tell them to do a great performance of a scene, you simply asked them to show you the idea. The giggles will go away once the material begins to develop and once the presentation process begins. If they do not go away then, it is time to start imposing rules of discipline and pressure for performance.

Piece by Piece.

In the early impros I give no emphasis at all to props, costumes or other theatrical embellishments. If someone grabs a prop and uses it, that is fine, but I try to keep everything to available items like chairs and maybe a table. If the group have been used to expressing themselves dramatically with the minimum of support items, you don't have to take anything away from them later. This places the creative emphasis on the ideas, characters and stories and on the ultimate aims of the play. It also places emphasis on clarity of expression, in ideas, words and actions. Props, effects, and costumes should only be added when the group decides they are essential.

As you gain playbuilding experience — and already from your knowledge of theatre — you will realise that none of these guidelines can be absolute. Creative work is not like that. You will also develop various techniques that suit your own style of working with young people.

JARGON

So, we have a few kids on their feet. They are showing us a scene that they have agreed is on the theme of the play. Some will do it with great 'realism' while others are less confident. Most will keep a careful eye on their 'audience' as they go. Some will play up to the group and others will hold back. The plot of the scene may get lost or may be presented so briefly that there is hardly anything there. But no matter how much or how little they show in the first impro, the play has started. Even if this scene is later thrown out of the play, the process of building has begun.

When that first impro is shown to the group you will then lead them into a critical discussion of the work and to a series of decisions about what to do with it. Immediately, you need language that will help all of you describe and assess the work, the drama. Avoid theatrical terms at this stage and avoid most discussion of performance abilities, which will receive attention in later workshops. Stress that the ideas, words and actions are what must be analysed. But do not use a word like 'analyse'. Develop a jargon for your group. You do that by using very vague terms to begin with. 'What did you think of that?' 'Let's look at the people in that scene.' 'Did that work?' 'Was that any good?' As these questions are answered and discussed, you and the group start to define your own terms. What does 'good' mean? What makes a piece of drama 'work'? After a while, you will have definitions, understood by all of you.

If you impose standard drama terms on the group, then you are demanding right answers and predictable responses. If the group says, 'We like it', then you are making progress, even if they do not know why they like it. Almost always they say, 'We like it, but . . .' and then suggest changes. This is the crucial part of the early work — the changes. And here the director must push for analysis and suggestions with some level of precision, despite the vague language you are all using.

A great deal of the discussion in the first five or six workshops will be based in the emotional responses of the group to the actual work and to the amazing process of seeing a play and a performance growing before their very eyes. Allow them their emotional responses and their vague intuition. But gradually press for more and more precision of thought and criticism and more precise use of language. Lead the way by being as precise as possible yourself about the strengths and problems of the scenes, while using the jargon you have created together. This is very difficult and requires you gradually to upgrade your own use of language while remaining in touch with the basic jargon. You must not become the know-all expert but you must not be so vague that you are no help to them.

I try always to bring my comments back to the logic of real-life, even if that sounds like a major paradox, and to the idea of audience re-action. 'I think people would laugh if you said that at that point. Do you want them to laugh?' 'Do you think a mother who has three kids to look after, a drunken husband and an invalid sister-in-law would really spend that much time talking to her parrot?' 'Do you want people to think life is really that depressing?' (This is one of my frequent questions to kids who often have a bleak view of the world we adults have created for them.)

In most cases the questions you ask will genuinely have at least two reasonable but very different answers. Often the questioning aims to clarify the intentions of the drama rather than change anything. Even in the early workshops the changes can be quite minor, a word or a gesture, as long as the discussion has pinpointed the purpose of the development before it is made. This process of analysing and honing every aspect of the creation seems slow at times but leads steadily to dramatic and performance strength. You must demand more and more careful analysis from the group as the process develops.

DRAMA KEYS

Part of your analysis will lie in identifying Drama Keys in each impro; keys that can be turned to unlock greater dramatic possibilities. (Another term I use for this process is 'pressure points' but I prefer the unlocking image.) The Drama Keys lie in the work created and also in the omission of possible developments. Is there any story twist that might be interesting? Is there any other character who could be let in at this moment? Is there anything that might be left out to give mystery or surprise? Are we telling too much or not enough?

In early workshops the director will be able to pick up more Drama Keys and make more developmental suggestions than most of the group. You must ensure that they all understand why you are wanting to unlock or lock with these Keys. Explain and get their permission to try the ideas, so that they begin to develop a knowledge of Drama Keys for themselves. Being able to identify and use Drama Keys will not only help them build better ideas into their plays but also help to build a better performance.

One of my favourite devices is the Diversion. I look at the scene for points where the story is flowing too easily, too clearly. I may then suggest bringing in a person to divert attention and maybe to set up two story-lines happening at once. This can then be developed so that each story enhances the other. A simple device is to introduce a much younger kid into a family scene. Dad and teenage Son are having a comfortable discussion in which the Son convinces Dad that he should leave school. In the face of inexorable logic, conveyed sensibly and calmly, the argument is won easily by the Son, who represents the group's view. But this is boring because it's too easy and undramatic. What if, early in the argument, we introduce the six-year-old Sister who is determined that Dad will fix her toy and forget older brother? The Sister screams and yells and throws tantrums. The Dad and Son try to carry on their sensible discussion. Dad yells for Mum to take the Sister away. Mum comes in and gets in the argument because she's too busy and she has had the kid all day and anyway, how come they are talking about the Son's entire future without her having a say in it? The Sister screams more. The Son gets angry. Dad gets angry. The arguments about leaving school are shouted, so they don't sound so sensible any more. Dad wants to talk about it some other time but Son demands an answer. Dad says no, no, no. Son storms out. Next time through we might add a Grandad to this scene to talk about how important education was in his day, and maybe an older sibling who is a scholar and on Dad's side; etc, etc.

The lines of the argument are still there but they now have a dramatic dynamic to them and a dimension of reality that says that many family decisions — many decisions — are based in emotion, not logic and are not always made under ideal conditions. Now, you must get group approval of these additions as you go because the scene inevitably changes quite a lot. In this case we have reversed the end-result of the scene. Is that useful to the play? Is it more true to life? Can we go on from there? We have made the argument more complex and the people more complex; the audience should like that. Goodies and baddies are not so clearly defined any more. Is that what the group wants? And if the play really needs Dad to say it's okay to leave school, that's easily fixed. Same scene but Dad gives in in despair and says, 'Yes, yes, yes'.

Sometimes the group wants to fantasise through the play that all things can be smoothly worked out and that the goodies and baddies are clear. Then you have to discuss the effect of the scenes and the ideas on the audience. In the argument example above, an audience will accept the developed version more readily because it fits with their experience of the world. It is also more easily performed because it fits with the group's experience of the world. The group — and the audience — will also respond to scenes that have a genuine dramatic energy to them. You will easily notice the scenes the group really enjoy doing. These are ripe for subtle development and will serve to lead the way in the growth of the play as the group enjoy the gradual improvement of their favourite scenes.

Another important Drama Key to use is the mood or tone of each scene. Sometimes young people find it hard to maintain a suitable tone, especially when their concentration is on story and character and ideas. You will be able to spot moments when an injection of humour could help to relieve a monotonous scene or to counterpoint the seriousness of a scene. Watch to see that the mood is appropriate to the basic dramatic purpose of the scene. I find that kids are good at injecting humour but sometimes it goes too far and there are jokes in a scene just for a laugh rather than to help the drama. You may have to encourage them to leave some of their favourite jokes out. Always explain this in terms of the dramatic needs of the play. Watch out for in-jokes too. These can be rejected on the basis of the audience's need to understand what's going on.

Drama seems to have its greatest impact at moments of strong contrast. You can help the power of the drama by showing the group how to use contrast of mood to emphasise a point. A lot can be done in the structuring of the play but it should also happen within scenes. Someone who makes a humorous crack just after being told a friend has died can be demonstrating an emotional reaction that is probably beyond their usual acting skill. This can also create a dramatic moment that will move and chill an audience. A person trying to make a serious point about peace while being laughed at by joking peers, can add a touch of emotionalism and zeal to statements that would not be acceptable in a 'straight' discussion about the issue.

The key-holes in a scene are the points where you can insert your Drama Keys to change a scene from a bald presentation of an idea or situation, into a dramatically satisfying representation. You have heard the term 'holes in the script', referring to a weak play. Well, those are simply key-holes that have not been filled with a Drama Key. Keep asking the group, 'how do we make an audience pay attention to the idea, think about it and care about it?' If the scene does not do those things then it has to be fixed up or scrapped. Each Scene, each step in the plot, each character, each idea must engage the audience's attention. Create a set of Drama Keys for yourself. You can draw from your knowledge of theatre, film, TV and literature. Mostly it is a matter of inventing solutions on the spot and of involving the whole group in seeking those solutions. Often you and they will be able to spot the hole in a scene without knowing which Key to use to fix it. Sometimes you may need to put a scene aside for a couple of sessions before returning to re-examine it.

Two common Drama Keys that I use are Explanation and Mystery. These can be used to control the pace of the drama. Mystery speeds things up and Explanation slows them down. The audience test is the best one here because the group can get so involved with what they are doing in the play that they forget that the audience does not know all the background discussions and research that the group knows. It is hard to decide just how much the audience should be told because explanations can easily become boring. But it is equally boring to be sitting there not knowing what is going on.

Sometimes I have found it necessary to have the group create a scene called The Explanation. These scenes never appear in the final play because that would be pretty dull. But the effect they have is to make it clear to us when we run though the play just how much explanation we need and just where it should go. With an Explanation Scene alongside the play we are able to judge how much of that content is already in the play and what pieces of the scene need to be retained. Placing the pieces of explanation into scenes can then be done on the basis of flow and pace. A sense of satisfying contrast can be achieved by placing quiet moments or passionate bursts of explanation into appropriate scenes. You must gauge how soon the audience needs to know certain information and place it accordingly.

The element of Mystery is the opposite to Explanation. Deliberate mystery can be dramatically very satisfying for an audience. It enhances the suspense and gives them a chance to use their own interpretative faculties. Look at each scene to see if too much is being revealed. Also look to see if there are moments when a sense of mystery could be invoked. The use of ambiguity is a form of mystery also. Of course, the insertion of mystery and ambiguity must be controlled tightly because you have spent so much time developing clarity of ideas and purpose in your playbuilding and you do not want to muddy the waters too much. Mystery and ambiguity are tools, or Keys and they must be used with clear purpose and accuracy.

THE LOCK-UP KEY

An important Key is the one that locks the scene up and says that it is now about as good as it is going to get. Better to do that too soon rather than too late. Once you have pushed a scene too far it is very difficult to retrieve it. This lock-up is on the content aspect of the scene and still allows improvements in the performance aspects. The scene will be run through in workshops so the group will keep feeling the dramatic strength of it. When the play gets into rehearsal and into the final structuring stages, any major weaknesses will show up and can then be repaired. You do not need to announce that a scene is now locked up; if you are asked, just let them know that it seems finished to you. Otherwise, simply leave the scene alone except for attention to performance detail.

OPENING AND CLOSING A SCENE

The most difficult jobs in improvising are how to start and how to end a scene. I do not worry much about this while people are on their feet because, once the substance of the scene is there, it is not hard to graft or edit in a sharp beginning and satisfying ending. Again, approach it from the audience point of view. Will this beginning draw the audience in? Will the beginning get them to the point of the scene quickly enough — or is it too quick? Will the ending leave the audience feeling satisfied — satisfied that the scene is whole and complete, even if all the questions have not been answered? Leaving the audience tantalised at the end of a scene can be very satisfying for them.

Often starts and ends of scenes will be there in the improvisation and it is just a matter of cutting away the excess material. Sometimes discussion will provide a solution and you try it out to ensure that it is dramatically sound. Look for your starts and ends in the early discussion about a scene. Often the person suggesting a scene will have a strong picture of how the drama starts and where they want it to go. Listen for that because the kids will not always recognise that they already have the structure. You may suggest a certain strong starting or finishing point: but make sure they are not falsely imposed. Improvisation can benefit greatly from having strong markers, giving the participants a springboard to strengthen the leap into the impro and a well-defined finishing line.

Providing a scene Framework from discussion before an impro starts can be a useful Drama Key in itself. The Framework should not be too elaborate. It will perhaps provide a start and an end, a central crisis statement and a specific entrance. Lots of combinations can be worked out, but four points should be the maximum so that enough freedom is allowed for the flow of the drama. (You may decide not to nominate an ending so that it can arise from the dramatic drive of the scene.)

'Feeling' for the ending of a scene is a very good method. This makes the end more satisfying to the group and often, more dramatically sound. 'Feeling' simply means running the scene and allowing the performers to use the dramatic impetus they develop to push them to an ending that feels complete. Working from the intuition of the performers gives the group the sense that you trust them and reminds them that the play is really in their hands. So, this is a good opportunity to encourage the intuitive aspects of drama: 'Let's not talk about it or think about it; let's just do it.' When the scene works there is an exhilaration from creating something from those vague, invisible sources inside us.

Starts and ends must hold within them the broad possibilities of linking with other scenes. The need to link scenes can also be used as a Drama Key to unlock possibilities not apparent when considering each scene singly. All these scenes must eventually link to provide a whole play and that point should be looked at each time a start or end is discussed.

THE PUNCHLINE

A strong Punchline to a scene is a most satisfying ending, particularly within episodic plays. Punchlines provide strength and clarity and add a sort of booster rocket for getting into the next scene. They can be used in the overall structure to give a firm dramatic drive to the piece and to vary pace. Carefully structured, punchlines can give an episodic play that sense of development to a climax that usually comes only in Story Plays. They can act as checkpoints for the main ideas. They are excellent ways of leaving an audience dramatically satisfied, or disturbed, or laughing, or sad.

LOGIC AND TWISTING AND PIVOTING

These Drama Keys can be used to steadily develop a clear scene, to change abruptly the direction of a scene or to inject humour and a bizarre point of view. Logic can be used for clarity and for mystery. By examining a scene from a logical stance the group can create a strong spine and a powerful sense of dramatic inevitability. A logical examination can also be used for the purpose of disturbing the audience by ignoring the surface logic and working to an internal logic of which the audience has insufficient knowledge. As long as the actions are true to some pattern of logic — revealed or not — the scene will have solidity. The works of Kafka are good examples of the use of unsettling logic. Even when we feel frustrated about the events in his books and stories, we still feel that structural strength that tells us there is a system at work. This is frightening because it is so mysterious. The same patterns and systems can be threaded into dramatic scenes.

The Twist and Pivot Keys are used to provide an anti-logic. Keep a lookout for moments — words or actions — when the drama can shoot off at tangents. This can provide humour — *The Goon Show, Monty Python* and Basil Fawlty do this constantly — or be used to unsettle a scene or to provide a new perspective. Twist and Pivot are valuable Keys in unlocking audience preconceptions about an idea or a character. *Baby Teeth* (see Chapter Seven) included a scene with Peter Pan who kept asking kids to jump on the wind's back and fly with him to Never Land. The kids reacted by saying he must be on drugs and by laughing at his weird costume. This unexpected reaction to a stock character allowed us to lead the audience into a deeper examination of childhood imagination. All I had to say was, 'Would modern kids· really go off with Peter Pan? What if they say no to him?'

THE 'WHAT IF . . .' QUESTION

The 'What if . . .' question is very useful. It covers many of the Drama Keys mentioned here and is a good non-aggressive way for the director to make suggestions. It immediately demands a felt or reasoned response and can easily lead to, 'Why don't we try it?' It is a good question to put when the creation has stalled, especially when a storyline is being developed. It is also a good question for stirring the group to reaction. 'What if Dad drops dead at this point because we can't seem to make him work in this play and that would . . .' By this time the group is reacting, yelling 'no!' probably, especially the person who plays Dad. You can insist on discussing the thought even though it may not be a real possibility, but in the discussion the group will raise issues that can then be fed back into solving the real problem.

There is nothing worse than everyone sitting about gloomily with no idea of how to unblock a dead-stop in the process. 'What if . . .' is a great unblocker and unlocker.

THE 'WHY NOT?' ANSWER

'Why not?' is also my favourite answer to suggestions in playbuilding. It demonstrates an attitude basic to successful playbuilding. The director and the group should always be working positively with every idea, finding ways to make things work rather than reasons why something won't work. 'Why not?' may cost a few minutes of trying out an unlikely idea at times, but it also unearths all kinds of good surprises. 'Why not?', as an answer, will help enormously in building a sense of creative freedom in your group. A real sense of creative freedom leads to an explosion of ideas and innovation.

A TITLE

If the play does not have a title to start with, it is important to get one as soon as possible. If this does not come easily, then you should allocate time to creating one before you go past the third or fourth workshop session. A title should be simple, obvious, a mystery that means a lot to the group, or a joke. The title gives the group this unique product: everyone can play football; everyone can study chemistry; everyone can do playbuilding; but only one group of people has a play called, 'Dirty Laundry', or 'The Life and Loves of Idi Amin', or 'Off-Key'. The title is like a password that only you and the group know. The sooner you have the password, the better the possibilities for a strong play.

TAKING NOTES

There comes a moment when it is clear that notes have to be kept about the ideas being offered and about the decisions made by the group. This will usually happen in the first workshop and it is a significant moment. It is another opportunity for the play to move into the hands of the kids. I always ask for one or two volunteers to keep records for the group. I explain that we do not need lots of notes, usually just the title of ideas or scenes will do, for example: 'The fish shop — Katie'; 'Argument with Dad over studying — Glenn'. Once created and in the play, these scenes might be listed in the scenario as 'Fish Shop' and 'Studying'. As you create scenes, so you also create a scenario, which is really just a list of scene titles which ends up being the full 'script' for the play. You need these scene titles for play-structuring, but they also have the same impact as the play title. They act as passwords into each scene. The shorter and simpler they are, the better.

It is vital that the kids make the notes for the play. They should be kept in a folder which will eventually contain any speeches written for the play, song lyrics, poems, found literary material, reference material, drafts of program and poster artwork, copies of letters about the project, etc. It can come to be quite a substantial file. During rehearsals the folder may be on your desk or in your bag, but everyone should have ready access to it. I have found that allowing one kid to look after the folder can result in real problems if that kid is sick or forgetful.

As the creation of the play continues, the list of scenes will grow and tentative scene-orders will occur. Photocopies of these lists should be given to each kid so that they have an increasing sense of development and see that they really are creating a play. Finally, that list of scenes should be posted back-stage or be on the playing area somewhere to give them confidence about what comes next. The final scene order is about the last thing decided upon so it will be the element least familiar to the group.

Do not push the group to write the play down. You might want to suggest the idea, for some specific purpose, once the play has been performed, but never before. Sometimes a group may be so in love with their play that some industrious soul will write it up later, but usually they want to move on to another play. One of the beauties of playbuilding is that the creative process is spontaneous and then fixed only by memory and commitment. Playbuilding does not put pressure on kids to 'act' but to 'present'. A script will bring all the problems of 'acting' to the fore — memorising words off a page; getting it 'wrong'; stage-fright; and a formality of performance that can stifle the natural creativity of kids. These things are avoided in playbuilding. The presentation/performance is natural and informal in feeling because the work belongs to the kids. Memorising is not a problem because it occurs session by session and is never made a chore. The playbuilding group cannot get the play 'wrong' because it is theirs. Anyway, the constant improvisations teach them to think on their feet and any 'mistakes' in performance are easily corrected as they go. I have never had any kid in any playbuilt show 'dry' or bring a performance to disaster. This comes, I am convinced, from that sense that this play is theirs and from their developed competence at improvisation.

The director will find it useful to keep notes on the workshops for his or her own use. I still do this from time to time. The notes should be written very soon after the workshop and they become a handy reference during the project, but even more useful some months or even a year later. As you develop your playbuilding skills, it helps to be able to examine your previous methods to see your own weaknesses and strengths. I shudder when I re-read some of my notes but they remind me that kids can create exciting plays despite almost anything the director does wrong, as long as there is a real atmosphere of creative freedom in the project.

SUMMARY

- The whole group participates in each improvisation — most as observers/critics/playwrights.
- Make early impros simple.
- Suggest to the group, 'Show me', to start impro. Never say, 'Act it.'
- Let impros drift and flow for as long as the participants want. Do not interrupt.
- Don't worry about giggles and poor concentration in early impros.
- Playbuilding is a process. Take many small, easily understood steps in developing scenes.
- Don't use props, costumes, etc. in early impros. Add things later, but only if absolutely necessary.

Jargon

- Use vague terms to discuss impros. Create a group jargon by gradually defining terms, as a group.
- In early impros, comment on performance should be minimal.
- Use the logic of real-life experience as a guide to analysing scenes.
- Use audience-reaction as a marker for discussing scenes.

Drama Keys

- Devise Drama Keys to unlock dramatic possibilities in scenes; the holes in a scene should be treated as 'key-holes'.
- *The Diversion* — Introduce characters or incidents to compete with the main drive of the scene.
- Adjust and contrast mood or tone of a scene to highlight dramatic moments.
- *Explanation and Mystery* — Add or subtract information in a scene to control pace and to keep the audience interested.
- *Lock-up* — Don't overdevelop a scene. Lock it in place when there is still some possible growth.
- *Opening and Closing Keys* — Analyse the various effects possible for starts and ends of scenes. Assess effects on audience needs. Keep the idea of linking scenes in mind when starts and ends are created.
- 'Feel' for endings through improvisation.
- *Framework* — Group-devising a framework of three or four points before an impro starts can add strength.
- *Punchlines* — For episodic plays especially, these provide clarity, strength and dramatic drive.
- *Logic* — Use for clarity and for mystery. Gives a strong back-bone.
- *Twist and Pivot* — To change audience perception; to add humour.
- 'What if . . .' draws debate and unusual solutions.
- 'Why not : . .' as suggestion and as answer to suggestion. Basic to playbuilding attitudes.
- Gain group approval of changes wrought by Drama Keys.
- *Title* — Find one early. It's the group password.

Taking Notes

- Let members of the group take all notes needed for the project.
- You keep the folder of notes, information and research material, but keep it somewhere accessible.
- Lists of scenes should be given to everyone as the play grows.
- Final scene order is their only script.
- Do not push to have the play written out/scripted *before* the performance; and only afterwards if the group is keen to do it.
- Keep personal notes to check your own progress.

THE TWINS VERSUS GENERAL INJUSTICE

This play began at Shopfront Theatre as an idea to be included in a group of plays for a specific festival on the theme of: 'Kids get into trouble and work their way out of it'. After some discussion a few decisions were made. The heroes had to be kids. We chose twins. Most 'troubles' we could think of seemed a bit TV-soapish. I suggested that the twins could be faced with general social injustice. A kid leapt on that idea and created our villain, General Injustice. We worked through the sorts of injustices with which kids might be confronted and there was much disagreement about whether things like school and the police were examples of injustice or were targets treated unjustly. Was Women's Lib really fighting against injustice or were they loonies? Was the family an unjust institution? What about Gay Lib? Should we support them, fight them, or laugh at them? How many liberation groups do we need?

The play became quite savage in its satire and some at Shopfront felt we had gone too far in criticising liberation groups as we did. But no subject should be beyond examination and the group felt that the play was fair and would certainly make audiences re-think their views on many of these issues. However, the group also decided that the play was not suitable for a festival atmosphere and the performances happened in the theatre at Shopfront.

The final 'script' for the play was a list of the major scenes as listed here, with some sub-headings for those scenes broken into smaller segments. The Narrator wrote out speeches for himself to introduce major scenes. The play is a good example of Twisting and Pivoting and of inverted logic taken to extremes. A number of devices used here are worth noting briefly as they will be dealt with at some length in later chapters.

Recorded Songs — I would now rarely use them; original music and songs, played live, are far more effective.

Repeating Patterns and Echoes — This play is full of them and it may be useful to refer back to it when reading that section in Chapter Six. The violence throughout became a choreographed pattern, providing a visual and thematic thread. Echoes such as the three 'applicant' scenes also strengthened the structure.

Balance and Contrast — Again useful to look back to this project when reading Chapter Six about these structural devices. The two family scenes here are good examples of the use of balance and contrast.

Blackouts — Note that there were none between scenes. The cast were allowed to control the flow, pace and structure of the performance.

Scenario for THE TWINS VERSUS GENERAL INJUSTICE

(Created and performed by: Kingston Anderson; Greg Bull; Cathy Burke; James Cooper; Louise Cooper; David Cummings; Stuart Hardy; Liz Hill; Cathy Janaway; Beverley Jay; Peter Warr; Chris Yallop; with E. B. as director. Produced at Shopfront Theatre.)

THE SET	Open space with a few chairs; entrances left and right at back. The songs were played over the action and one was mimed by General Injustice. The scenes flowed into one another without blackouts. The Narrator spoke from off-stage, over the sound system.
'SINGING IN THE RAIN'	Gene Kelly sings and a small girl dances happily. General Injustice, in battle-helmet, army boots and greatcoat, enters with an umbrella with which he covers the girl, while leering at the audience. She screams.
INTRODUCTIONS	The Narrator introduces the Twins — wholesome and cheery — and General Injustice — who waves to the audience, letting the girl escape — and warns of the dreadful tale of horror and adventure that is to follow.
SEVEN DEADLY SOCIAL DISEASES	Narrator introduces these with great melodrama. — Valium bottles dance and sing, 'When my baby smiles at me I go to Rio'.

— Rape by leap. An older boy is leapt on by a cute young girl.

— General Injustice enters with a white cane and in dark glasses. As he crosses stage, information about V. D. from the phone information service is played.

— School. Brief burst by a Hitlerian teacher.

— Violence. Mum keeps slapping her small child, saying, 'How dare you humiliate me in public.'

— Narrator warns that blatant sexual activity is to follow. Group does calisthenics, leered at by General Injustice.

— Religion. 'Are you going to church on Sunday?' 'No, I can't afford it.'

— TV and especially hairy chests. A boy with a horribly hairy chest sings, 'When my baby smiles at me I go to Tempe, Tempe Station.'

— The Motor Car. A policeman arrests a driver for picking his nose on a public highway.

TWINS HOME LIFE   All is sweetness and light in exaggerated performance style. The kids are excellent at school, sports and all the creative arts, are clean and healthy and love everybody. Mum loves housework. Dad is a banker who helps lots of people. They eat apple pie and have singalongs around the piano.

DAVID AND THE POPPY SEEDS   David takes the cow to sell and two men in dark glasses give him some magic poppy seeds for it. His mother beats him for being stupid and throws the seeds away. During the night the seeds grow very high and so does David, who dances amongst the poppies. His mother tries to chop down the poppies but David chops his mother up. The poppies dance away when David's father arrives. Dad realises David is on drugs and that he has neglected the boy so he takes him to the pub to have a talk with him. David asks, 'Am I a man now, dad?'

INTERVIEWS FOR MEDICAL SCHOOL   Prospective medical students are rejected or accepted for reasons of social backgrounds.

PROTEST MOVEMENTS   Gay Lib members save a boy from being bashed up by beating up the basher with handbags.

— A stirring Women's Lib speech demands that men must be 'disarmed' to prevent violence against women. Shears and large scissors are gathered during the speech.

— A flasher runs into the Women's Lib meeting and flashes. A girl grabs scissors and 'disarms' him.

— General Injustice dedicates a song to 'coloured folk' and sings, 'Mammy'. He is hit in the face with a cream pie.

— A boy handing out religious pamphlets is beaten up. He screams for more.

— General Injustice offers a little boy a boiled lollie. The boy says, 'Not today, mister. I've got a headache.'

— A rape is occurring under a blanket — Two pairs of bare feet stick out. Other boys are lined up, waiting their turn. Women's Lib beat up all the boys and rescue the rapee who is also a boy.

WINDOW DRESSER INTERVIEWS   Unlikely candidates try for the job.

THE BAD FAMILY   Liz is beaten up by her teacher. At home, James is having a shoot-out with the police. Mum makes him give up because he really does like jail where he is continually beaten and raped. Dad smashes his car into the house and comes in, knocks Mum down and drags Liz off to the bedroom. Mum reminds them that 'The Brady Bunch' is on TV so they return to watch it.

	Liz sees her grandma in the audience and shoots her, saying, 'I hate old people.'
POLICE BRUTALITY	Protesters outside police station are upset by a policeman who calls them names like 'naughty people'. The policeman is played by the nine-year-old. When only the Protest Leader is left the cop shoots him in the knees and beats him up.
RED-HEAD LIBERATION	The Red-head, hiding his hair most of the time in a beanie, is spurned by all, made fun of and beaten up. He is saved by the Twins, leading Red-head Lib.
LIVE SHOW	Two TV Sets (in box costumes) watch a live, 'arty' dance. They pick the dancer up and shake him because he's out of focus. They get bored and beat the dancer up because there's not enough violence in live shows.
DEVIANT SEX	Two nice young people enter as the Narrator warns the audience to watch this scene closely for disgusting sexual activities. The boy and girl are at a bus stop and with many huge pauses they have a very shy and innocent conversation. He finally asks her out and she says he'll have to speak to her dad about it. He says all right, he will. General Injustice rushes on screaming that it's filthy and perverted.
'I'M NORMAL'	A popular song of the time, mimed by General Injustice with a chorus line of boys. The song tells of all kinds of perversions but to General Injustice this is normal.
DOLE INTERVIEWS	Very different applicants for the dole are rejected with bureaucratic language.
'ALL MY FRIENDS ARE GETTING MARRIED'	This popular song was played behind the scene. The Twins are in love and rather ashamed because Cathy is pregnant. They discover that they were really adopted and can marry after all. General Injustice appears, thinly disguised, as a priest and marries everybody in all sorts of combinations. He then chases the Red-head from his church.
'SINGING IN THE RAIN'	Big finish with all the cast dancing happily as plastic snow floats from the ceiling.

CHAPTER 4

'ALL THE WORLD...' INCLUDING EVERYTHING IN THE PLAY

Many other building elements can go into creating a play besides improvised scenes. Encouraging your group to include a range of their skills, borrowed items and material other than words will add texture and variety to the play. Anything that belongs to or is created by the group is easily assimilated, but some care needs to be taken with borrowed material.

Once some sessions of improvisation have occurred, you should encourage the group to seek out other ways of expressing the ideas and other material relevant to the play. This activity will not only add directly to the content bulk of the play but will also bring the group to look at the ideas from different viewpoints. Sometimes I will bring in for discussion quotes or items from newspapers relevant to the topic. If the group want to include such material in the play, then we have to find ways to do that without making it appear like an academic footnote.

INDIVIDUAL SKILLS

If anyone in the group has a performance or creative skill, dancing; juggling; playing a musical instrument; singing well; composing; acrobatics; etc., the director should know about it within the first few workshops. Not every skill can be included in every play, but skills can be grafted on quite blatantly if the group wants that.

In *S.K.Y.* someone's ability to draw provided a means of linking some of the scenes. In *The Playground Play* (Chapter Five) a boy's ability to play the tuba was used when we needed an attention-getting device. In *Double Cubed* with Cleveland Boys' High, a boy's ability to play the trumpet was used to add noise and humour to scenes — 'God Save The Queen' on trumpet is funny — as well as to make a major point about parental support for even a tiny musical talent.

Be very careful that young people are not presented as skilled performers and then allowed to look foolish. A good tap-dancer can be given a solo spot; a mediocre tap-dancer can be part of a larger scene. Weaving the acquired skills of your group into the statement of the play makes the play even more clearly the voice of that group. It also enables kids to demonstrate considerable skill levels within the play and that will increase their confidence in the overall work.

PHYSICAL CHARACTERISTICS

Young people — especially teenagers — are often acutely conscious of their own physical qualities. Often they see their physical selves in very negative ways and comments about this will come up in discussions and in scene creation. Using the tallness, shortness, fatness, prettiness, etc. of the performers can emphasise the group's ownership of the play and can make them aware of using their physicality creatively. This is fraught with obvious dangers and must be approached positively and sensitively.

In *The Twins versus General Injustice* the running gag about the red-head arose from the redheaded boy's own stories about the way he was mistreated because of his red hair. In *Childmyth* a lot of the structure of the play came from the fact that we had three blond boys of similar looks but of different ages and heights. They looked rather like the same person at different stages of growth, so we used that. In *How to use a machete in a Concrete Jungle* with J.J. Cahill High School, a scene derived from one kid's strong European accent.

In *Two Nice Kids* at Shopfront Theatre, a long scene was created about teenage feelings of physical inadequacy. The scene was quite poignant as well as funny because the two teenagers were particularly attractive and would seem to have no reason to worry about their physical selves. However, both the girl and the boy revealed their fears of acne and body odour, as well as their hatred of various features — freckles; small nose; big feet; teeth; etc. Both characters were shown to suffer from loneliness caused by fear of inadequacy and not from their actual appearance. Many adults who saw the scene commented on how many awful memories it brought back.

In *Double Cubed*, there was a moving scene based around a boy's obesity. He was egged on by his friends to ask out a girl he liked — Doreen. But whatever George said to Doreen, she simply said, 'You're fat, George.' George gave her presents and she said, each time, 'You're fat, George.' When his friends asked him what Doreen had said, George told them, 'She said I'm fat.' While I had gone to some trouble to ensure that George was really prepared to perform this scene, I have reservations now about whether it was rather too much like psychodrama. The scene certainly had a strong honesty and impact and all the cast, including George, felt the power of it. But, given that project again, I think I would discourage the group from using the scene.

SONGS AND MUSIC

Nowadays most of my playbuilt shows include songs. They encapsulate mood and emotion powerfully and provide the group with excellent tools for the expression of elevated emotion. Young, untrained performers who in the main do not want to be actors find it difficult to convey the more subtle and powerful emotional elements of a play through their performance talent alone. Songs, mime, dance and the use of dramatic contrast can construct the emotion of a scene, enabling the kids to present their ideas powerfully and beautifully.

Anyone can sing, and no kid should be deprived of the pleasure of singing in a show. This does not mean that everyone can sing equally well but everyone can sing in the group numbers. It is how the singers and the song are presented dramatically that matters. The singing should become one more method of presenting the play's views and ideas, rather than a moment for skill, unless you have a particularly gifted singer. One boy I worked with was ashamed that he had been the only person in his school musical not allowed to sing. That's an awful thing to do to someone. He later toured schools with our Shopfront version of *The Tempest*, which included many songs. He was not a great singer but he did a good job of presenting songs on stage. I sympathise because I was kicked out of my school choir as a bad singer — and I love singing.

Because music and songs are such powerful dramatic tools, I am opposed to using recorded songs and music for a playbuilt show. I have done it but have almost always regretted it. The major reason is the very strength of a song. Anything with that much impact ought to be the invention of the group. Borrowing speeches or quotes or poems is not quite as overwhelming as a recorded song can be, and in the case of most other borrowings they are still presented by the kids as performers. When a song is played over the sound system it takes on a disembodied and 'cold' performance quality while the rest of the play is 'warm', flesh and blood performance. If a song by someone outside the group must be used then it should be performed by the group. The same applies to music composed outside the group — play it live if possible. However, recorded music as background is not really so harmful if carefully chosen so that it does not swamp the creativity of the group.

Recorded songs are almost always chosen because somebody in the group thinks the song says just what the play is trying to say, or because the song moves them. Including a song that moves you, or the group, very easily becomes maudlin self-indulgence. Letting a recorded song speak for the group can look like poverty of imagination. It also becomes a statement beyond the control of the group. Too often we assume that an audience will share our response to a favourite deep-and-meaningful song, but there is no way to control that reaction.

When the performers allow the flow and voice of the play to be transferred from themselves to a recording, they lose the performer/audience bond that is the stuff of theatre itself, and the same applies to miming and dancing. A playbuilt play has its own style and standards. The situation is not quite so bad if the songs are being used for humorous purposes. Then they become more like sound effects behind a comic point. But even here great care must be taken. I think that even a very ordinary song written and performed by the group within the context of a good playbuilt show will have greater impact on an audience and greater strength with the play than a recorded song. The style and quality of the group's song is also more readily structured into the overall play. Of course, in theatre it is hard to lay down absolute rules. No doubt you can quote occasions on which recorded songs seemed to add wonderfully to a group-created play. But I prefer to risk everything on the kids in my group. They need the creative exposure more than the recording star does.

If someone in the group can play guitar or flute or piano or even mouth organ, you should be able to get some songs together, but it is very hard to write a really good song that is exactly right for the play. The music is often less difficult because we are not looking for great music but for performable music. If you are lucky enough to have a really good composer of songs in the group, the quality and impact of the play increases markedly.

In several of my playbuilt shows I was fortunate in having Martin Blacker, a very talented young song-writer, compose the music. He also brought considerable music-performance skills to the shows. His special gift, in song-writing, lay in understanding just how much the composer needed to give to the songs. He knew that the music had to be a tool for the group to use. He knew it had to carry the ideas and words rather than make an impact as brilliant music. He also was able to make allowance in his music for the fact that the songs would usually be performed by non-singers. In one show he and I wrote a song called, 'This is a Song for Someone Who Can't Sing.' In brief, he was a pragmatic musician who wrote and played the music that a show and a group needed, always, of course, at a standard a bit higher than the group really imagined they could reach. It is possible to write songs as a group — especially the words — but it is difficult and often leads to great arguments about the music. There are so many different schools of thought about music amongst young people and the arguments can prove frustrating when all you want is a simple tune to lift a set of words to performance level; a performance level that can be reached by non-singers.

Song-writing, like speech-writing, seems to be an activity for one or for a partnership. In play-building, group input before and after the event is assumed. My own method has usually been to write the words myself and find someone within the group who can write the music. I enjoy writing

Liz Hill in the hands scene, *Shore Sines*.

words for songs and I know that the playbuilding process will ensure group input and discussion about all the songs. I also ensure that kids in the group have every opportunity to do the job if they wish and my groups will often choose to turn existing poems into songs. With longer songs, the group and I will map out in some detail what the song needs to say before I write anything. With shorter songs, a discussion about the mood and the central idea is enough. Once I have written the words I then show them to the group for consideration and changes. With Martin and with one or two others who wrote music quite rapidly, we might take words and music to the group together and test the whole song out on them. In every case, words and music have to go through the same editing and analysis process to which all the material is subjected. If you are writing the words or music yourself, then you must be sure the group is confident enough to be able to tell you they don't like your work. You should be a creative part of the group but you must also take care not to abuse your position.

QUOTES AND POEMS

These can be very useful in supporting the ideas of a play. In the case of a poem, skilful placement can give considerable emotional impact, control and contrast. Because these borrowings are performed by the group there is not the same danger as in using recorded songs, but do take care that the device is not overdone. There may be occasions when a whole range of quotes and poems can be carefully placed to illustrate a vital point or a major issue. In the scenario of *The Playground Play* you will see how we did this to give credibility and force to Kids Rights issues. The group's ideas about young sexuality — a touchy issue — were presented in this play almost entirely through the words of Shakespeare and William Blake. This was a powerful combination and it was hard for an audience to reject the scene without at least some serious thought.

Borrowed quotes and poems should be acknowledged, whenever possible, within the play itself. This can be done quite plainly: " 'Infant Sorrow' by William Blake", then read the poem. Acknowledgement adds an extra touch of honesty to the play and tells the audience clearly what is borrowed

Totem hospital scene from *Shore Sines*.

and what is original. Sometimes, in the case of very well-known material, this may not seem necessary, but I have always felt that due acknowledgement within the play lends a nice touch of care and respect; all copyright material must of course be acknowledged in the program.

POEMS AND SPEECHES

Although a playbuilt show is not written down, there is no reason why writers in the group cannot use their own material or write material specifically for the play. There are good reasons to encourage them. But anything that is written by one or more kids must go through analysis and discussion sessions like everything else. I try to read in advance any work submitted to the group so that I can support the writers if necessary. Sometimes, if it is not good or suitable, I will suggest that it be re-written before being presented for group discussion.

In the case of a small speech or poem, I always suggest that the author should perform it in the play and that it should be read from a piece of paper. This saves the kid from all those memory nerves and tells the audience, 'This is my own work.' Sometimes the performer will announce, as he or she unwraps the piece of paper, 'This is a poem I wrote about . . . ' Producing the actual document on which this created statement is written has a strong effect of immediacy on an audience and tends to add focus.

WRITING SCENES

Sometimes one or more kids will want to write a scene and I always say, 'Why not?' I do have a lot more faith in playbuilding a scene than in a written version, but sometimes a scene can become complex and writing it down can clarify an issue. Sometimes an idea brought up in discussion will appeal to a writer in the group and they will make a special plea to be allowed to write it. Again, why not? I must admit to feeling obliged to encourage anyone who wants to write anything any time.

Sometimes an experienced group will ask me to write a scene for them. This can only happen after lots of work has been done on the scene in improvisation and if there are specific problems which could be solved by committing it to paper. If a group knows you and trusts you they will know that you can bring an objective eye to the work and be able to translate a troublesome scene into words and actions that they will recognise as their own. Of course, the work must be rigorously analysed by the group and their criticisms accepted.

Although I say, 'Why not?' to requests for written material to be included in a playbuilt show, I try to ensure that the group is not just trying to avoid a difficult impro. I also draw the line on how much writing can be in a play before the play is virtually a full script — a different beast altogether. Any more than two scenes being written would seem pretty damaging to the playbuilding concept of a project. And there is a limit to how often in a play the audience can cope with performers producing bits of paper and reading their works. We are looking at a play, after all, not a poetry reading. All this is largely a matter of commonsense and improvising is mostly more fun than writing. Any excess of written material can be edited out in the final structuring of the play.

DANCE AND MOVEMENT

With new groups the expression of ideas tends to remain verbal. I keep the possibility of dance and movement alive in workshops, but new playbuilders are often a bit suspicious of those forms. The inclusion of some aspects of the theatre and dramatic arts will often depend on the knowledge and enthusiasm of the director, and I confess to being a bit of a movement 'dunce'. However, because of this, I do make an effort to compensate and most groups doing their second show with me will create a dance or movement piece within their play.

Dance need not be presented as a series of technical exercises any more than singing need be. If kids can walk then they can dance. I've even seen wonderful people create dance with kids confined to wheelchairs. I take dance to be rhythmical movement, usually to music, that uses the movement of all the body, not only the feet. Like singing, dance can help a play control and contrast strong emotional impact. Dance can also give kids the chance to look and feel quite beautiful in their play.

Devising movement — which I take to be a stylisation of normal body movement, usually without music — can be easier for a group to handle and I often find that an effective movement scene in a play will lead to a good dance scene in the next play for that group. I also view a tableau as a version of movement, movement frozen into a dramatic moment. A tableau can be a very effective ending to a scene. Stylisation of movement in a play adds a dimension of drama beyond the realistic and the expected. It also allows the group to manipulate their audience's viewpoint so that the other material in the play can be seen from a different perspective. Patterns and relationships can be displayed through movement, enhancing the verbal elements of the play and offering an expression of ideas and themes in a fresh and dynamic way.

MIME AND SILENT ACTION

Mime also tends to be one of those very theatrical things that kids assume they cannot do and that looks a bit arty. For this reason I usually use silent action with new groups and let that develop into mime for later shows. The use of mime does require real discipline and a high level of skill, if it is to be successful. Unlike singing and dancing, mime requires more than joyous enthusiasm to look all right. But mime does bring such an unusual perspective to a scene and can be so beautiful as a skill that it is worth the trouble.

It is possible to create an entire playbuilt show using mime. One of my colleagues at Shopfront, Faye Westwood, built a show called, *Concrete Sox*, entirely through mime. It dealt with teenage problems and the heightened emotional impact of the miming was exactly right for the intensity of the subject matter. Mime, when it is very well done, can cope with the use of recorded music and songs as background, though I would recommend great care and deliberation in the choice of music. In *Concrete Sox*, the choice of popular music to accompany scenes of teenage distress worked well, but mainly because the standard of the mime work was excellent.

The idea of silent action is a natural step towards mime but does not require stylisation and the same skill control. *Dancing With Kangaroos* (see Chapter Eleven) used silent action extensively. Suggest to the group occasionally that they do not need all the words and that they should let a scene run in silence, using actions to show the mood and relationships within the scene. This helps your performers to develop a sense of contrast, so that they feel the power of putting silence and shouting alongside each other and learn the way a natural movement or gesture can speak more eloquently than words.

TECHNICAL EQUIPMENT

Within the play itself it can be useful and effective to have televisions, tape-recorders, slide-projectors, etc. These can certainly bring another dimension of expression to the material in the play. Often they can be used to express the actuality of a situation, by showing or re-playing the factual material. Technical equipment can be particularly effective in a documentary play.

In a play at Shopfront, a series of slides of the cast as young children was used. The flashback scenes to the younger years and experiences of the cast were greatly enriched by the slides in a way that the group could never have achieved with performance alone. In a play called *Replica*, about consumerism, done at Shopfront, the director, Monita Roughsedge, created several mock TV commercials with the cast and showed these with videotape on a TV set placed very effectively within the stage-set.

Ensure that any technical wizardry you use works efficiently and take care that the play does not rely too much on it. This is even more important when it comes to directing the show and the use of lighting, sound, etc (more of that in a later chapter). I reiterate my view that the successful running of the play and the successful presentation of the material by people is preferable to a lot of technology.

DON'T INCLUDE EVERYTHING!

There are limits to how kaleidoscopic a play should be. There can come a point where the piece looks overloaded with clever tricks. Keep a balance. A straightforward play with no added song, dance, mime, poem or technical gadgetry can be perfectly satisfying if the ideas are good and they are presented with strength and commitment.

The more the group can be seen as the people who are controlling this amazing event — this play created out of nothing but their own imaginations — the more excited the audience will be and the more praise they will shower on the kids. The more the kids have contributed, the more they will gain in self-esteem, confidence, skill, etc. There is nothing quite so exciting as a simple tight-rope walk — no gimmicks, just the suspense of wondering if the walker will slip or will reach safety. Give the kids their chance to walk the tight-rope of a whole play with no gimmicks, no wires attached, no safety net

— well, not any that the audience can see, anyway. Be really daring! Believe in the young people you are working with. Let the play rest on the human presence and worth of the kids. Let their ideas and their abilities succeed, undisguised.

SUMMARY

- Encourage groups to seek a variety of methods of expressing and demonstrating their ideas.
- If kids have individual skills — dancing; juggling; music; etc. — encourage inclusion of these in the performance.
- Use songs, mime, dance and dramatic contrast to construct the emotion of a scene, rather than relying on 'amateur acting'.

Songs and Music
- Each song is a scene in itself.
- Anyone can sing! And, at worst, anyone can be helped to perform a song if they want to do it.
- Avoid use of recorded songs. They can be acceptable as background if care is taken to avoid swamping the work of the group.
- Songs created by the group are powerful tools. Keep the music simple.
- The director can be involved as creator of words or music for a song but only if the ideas are group-created and if full and open analysis of the results is ensured.

Quotes and poems
- Acknowledge in the performance the source of borrowed material.
- If kids ask to write material for the play, encourage them.
- Material written by an individual performer should be read by him or her from a sheet of paper.
- Writing of scenes can be encouraged if suggested by the group, but don't let this be a cop-out from improvising difficulties.

Dance and movement
- Develop from silent, natural movement into dance and/or mime.
- The tableau can be a useful device to end or begin a scene.
- Keep the show in the control of humans and in a human rhythm.
- Do not overwhelm a play with gimmickry and dramatic devices.

OVERGROWN and SHORE SINES

Both these projects set out to use a wide variety of performance elements in exploring their themes. With *Overgrown* we wanted a play that would bring the whole membership of Shopfront together in a display of their skills. The theme and title of *Overgrown* were chosen because there had been much discussion in the media about Sydney becoming too big and about Australia's natural environment being abused. One kid commented that we wanted the bush to be overgrown but didn't want the city to be overgrown.

Shore Sines was created by the first Shopfront overseas touring group. The major touring show was *The Shopfront Collection*, a compilation play, that included scenes and songs from many Shopfront shows. While these were mostly playbuilt scenes, they did not represent the performers' own creative work. We chose to include dance, masks, music, songs and mime in *Shore Sines* as these represented skills that the group had and we also wanted to show the scope of playbuilding on a theme.

Notes for OVERGROWN

(Created at Shopfront Theatre with a cast of over forty young people of widely different ages, using three directors.)

I can only give some broad notes about this show as a scenario was not kept and my memory is not detailed enough to give a complete breakdown of scenes. The play was a full, two-act, playbuilt show, nearly two hours long. Because we dealt with city and rural issues, most aspects of the show came in pairs. Each act had a major dance piece, a puppet show and songs, as well as the dramatic scenes. One half of the set represented the city and the other half a jungle. A raised stage in between became a meeting place for ideas and held a large, wooden puppet theatre which also doubled as a TV set.

The play began with an overture played by a small orchestra. The first puppet show — a shadow-puppet play — was called, 'The Omelette that Ate Carlton' and was a horror-show spoof. At the end, the kids of the area saved Carlton by eating the omelette with lashings of tomato sauce. The two major dance pieces were choreographed to represent the bustle of the city and the freedom of the country. There were many short satirical scenes on matters as diverse as gnomes, scorpions and Tarzan. A series of scenes dealt with a city family who found a 'wolf-boy' while they were on a picnic. They took him home and taught him to be civilised. When he was finally civilised enough to see what was happening in the world, he committed suicide. This was a rather bleak message in amongst the variety and fun of the rest of the show.

The blending of the different forms of performance proved very successful and provided a rich and entertaining show. The organisation was enormous, but is possible in a school where a number of different teachers can offer their skills. The rewards for the group are great because they see their own skills and interests being woven into a much larger performance tapestry and each sub-group learns from the others. Interest in dance and puppetry grew considerably at Shopfront after the performances of *Overgrown*.

Scenario for SHORE SINES

(The play was sub-titled, 'A play about totems and symbols.' Cast and creators were — Karina Andjelic; Scott Berry; Martin Blacker; Liz Hill; Rohan Love; Kris Plummer; Francine Sparre; and Erin Vincent, with E.B. as director.)

The set consists of four chairs, a stand for hanging costumes and a cymbal on a stand. Most props are laid out on the floor at the back. The cast stay on-stage throughout. A large square cloth and some significant props, e.g. a skull and some masks, are positioned on stage at the beginning.

WORDS   At the start there are cards on the floor with various spellings of 'shore'

	and 'sines' on them. Kris picks these up as she gives the dictionary definitions. The others use stylised movement to suggest some of the definitions. When Kris defines 'sign' as 'mark traced on surface', she draws a circle on Scott's face.
ACTOR 1	Scott who is dressed in black leotards and black top — holds a skull in Hamlet pose. The others pick up masks and form a tableau representing grieving over a dead body. Scott watches this and makes the 'O what a peasant rogue am I' speech from *Hamlet*.
ZODIAC DANCE	Martin, Karina and Rohan play music as others dance. The dance was choreographed by the dancers. At intervals a performer steps forward with a quote about the stars and with lists of people born under certain star signs. These lists tend to make fun of the star-sign idea, e.g. Doris Day and Adolph Hitler are both Aries; Queen Victoria, Bob Dylan and John Wayne are all Geminis.
GUN 1	Kris, Karina and Rohan each hold up a gun. Kris has an antique gun which she sees as a beautiful work; Rohan likes the symbolism of power; Karina sees a symbol of evil.
ACTOR 2	Scott recites, 'What a piece of work is man'.
MUSIC	All the group form an orchestra and play a piece of music composed by them as a group. The piece includes many small percussion instruments.
'O, BRAVE NEW WORLD'	As music finishes, Karina steps forward and recites that speech from *The Tempest*.
HANDS	Liz puts on a red nose and a pair of silver gloves. As Martin conducts a comic orchestra, she performs a list of hand gestures, e.g. Sshh; come here; stop; thumbs up and down; on the nose; who cares; don't know; hot stuff; etc.
LANGUAGE	Scott recites short piece from Shakespeare: 'You taught me language; and my profit on it is, I know how to curse.'
THE BALLAD OF THE PENGUIN AND THE LION	This scene was also used in Piece by Piece and is detailed in Chapter Eleven.
DANCE/BIRTH	To choreography by the group; music played by Martin. Erin wears a gold cloak and mask and represents some goddess of birth. She helps three of the others into the world. Each has a 'life' dance. As they grow, Erin encourages them to leave the nest. Scott doesn't want to go and has to be forced out. As the music finishes, Erin turns to the audience and slowly removes her mask as the others take off her cloak.
'COME TO DUST'	Words from Shakespeare's *Cymbeline*; music by Scott Berry. Scott and the girls sing the song. 'Golden lads and girls all must, As chimney-sweepers, come to dust.'
TOTEM HOSPITAL	Martin and Rohan, dressed as doctors, introduce the scene. 'Totem Hospital — The television series where the case histories are true. Western society has lost touch with the totems and sacred symbols of our tribal pasts. Totem Hospital offers the cure.'
	(Note: This scene was developed through intensive workshopping and editing. At one point in the process it was twenty-five minutes long. It was very funny and bizarre but performed quite seriously.)
	Mr Ridgididge is a patient who lies across two chairs in a rigid state. Nurse Lushley enters and dusts him off with a feather duster, giving extra attention to the genital area. Mr Ridgididge looks out at the audience and screams silently. He keeps doing this throughout the scene. Matron,

tippling from her flask, sits on Mr Ridgididge who falls to the floor in a stiff, but now bent, heap. Matron thinks that he has made a pass at her. He slowly crawls towards the audience for the rest of the scene as the others rush about him. Matron drinks constantly and argues with everybody. Every time the words, 'Totem Hospital', are said, the whole cast look out into the audience and speak as with one voice. Mr Ridgididge mouths the words. Kris brings her daughter, Karina, to the hospital. She is in shock. Her mother has thrown out all her rabbit's feet and other good-luck tokens. The doctors call in a Specialist, who is Francine. She is from the Zippaloola tribe and a totems expert. She declares that the girl had T.O. — Totem Overload — due to all the symbols her mother had heaped on her. Specialist opens her bag and takes out a teddy bear which she keeps consulting about the case. The Specialist waves a skull over Karina's bed and Karina goes into hysterics. Specialist announces that this is a case of T.D.S. — The Totem Deprivation Syndrome — and everyone keeps muttering T.D.S. The Specialist announces it is time for S.T. — Sock Therapy. She takes some long, dirty socks from her bag and whirls them about Karina's head, chanting. Karina recovers while the others are gagging from the smell. Karina makes a speech about never relying on symbols, etc. again; she will be independent and free, etc; 'touch wood'. The Specialist goes off, talking to teddy. Matron grabs Mr Ridgididge and tells him how he is the only one who has ever understood her. He screams silently as Martin finishes off, 'Just another day at . . . Totem Hospital.'

GUN 2   Rohan comes forward with a gun and makes a pro-gun speech. 'Guns don't kill people; people kill people. ' He says that guns are a symbol of security. The girls all hold guns to Rohan's head and ask, 'Feeling secure?' They walk him to the back.

'TOMORROW AND   Martin and Scott begin singing this song; words from *Macbeth*, with
TOMORROW AND   music by Martin. The others put out all the symbols used in the play so that
TOMORROW'   the stage area is littered with symbols. The rest of the cast join in the song, finishing, 'It is a tale Told by an idiot, full of sound and fury, Signifying nothing.'

CHAPTER 5

STRUCTURING I
EACH PROJECT; EACH WORKSHOP; EACH SCENE

Teachers will be familiar with the practice of structuring a lesson; directors will be familiar with structuring a rehearsal. Both will be aware that successful structuring of lesson or rehearsal should be within a larger structuring that will lead to successful performance — in an exam, an assessment or a production. These same lines of structuring should be adopted in every playbuilding project. Perhaps the most important thing to remember about the structural elements of a playbuilding project is that all of them should eventually be under the control of the group. Real structural knowledge and power must be passed to them. It is this coming to grips with structure that seems to me the most powerful benefit and the most useful skill to be gained from playbuilding.

Structure must be attended to at all stages and levels of the project. This includes structuring the relationship of the director to the group. The director should structure that relationship through a series of steps — initiator; leader; encourager; approver; expert; critic at all times; equal creator; teacher of skills; director; outsider.

The ideal director structure is that of gradually rubbing yourself out of the project. Even those pieces you have contributed should have blended so well with the rest of the play that everything will belong to the group. This situation can be very difficult because your own ego and pride will be on the line. But you will have to be content with the approval of those peers who know what this playbuilding job is all about, while the kids in your group become more and more convinced that you had practically nothing to do with the play; maybe even been a bit of a nuisance at times. You should start out as one of the group — 'We're all going to create this terrific show' — that evolves to the point where you will be advising them and directing them in their show, and finally they will be asking you, as a friend of the group and one whose opinion they value, what you think of their play and their performances.

So that this split can become complete, the director must structure the project to ensure that his or her presence is not needed at all for the performances. No ego-desperate hanging on by making yourself the stagemanager or by playing music for them or even by running the lights and sound. No! Your job — except as a director giving notes to the cast — is over and out and the show is theirs; all theirs. If you do cling on you will diminish their level of achievement and all the benefits they should gain from the project.

This is not to underestimate the importance of the director when the show is finally in performance, but the role is different and will seem quite separated from the group. It is vital that you press the group to continue analysing and criticising their work and, with a play that will run for several performances, to make changes to the play as a result of their interaction with an audience. The project is not over until all performances have been done, any follow-up benefits have been achieved (such as videotaping the show, etc.) and a final assessment has been carried out by you and the group. Once the first performance has happened, your voice becomes that of an objective — though caring and knowing — critic. But your voice is only one of many they will be hearing — friends, relatives, teachers, other directors, general audience members, etc. This means that your voice must now be at its clearest and be logically and carefully critical, if you are going to keep the group on line to assess their work effectively.

When I led the first overseas tour for Shopfront to youth theatres in the United Kingdom, we took two group-created plays which had been worked on for some months and then performed for a season in Sydney before the tour. In our first three performances overseas, audiences raved about the work, really did fall off their seats with laughter and crowded around for autographs after shows. This was fairly heady stuff, but as a group we continued our practice of analysing the work and before our performances in Liverpool — our fourth stop — we made major changes to both plays. We changed the order of scenes and dropped two scenes in one show. With the other show, we made changes to eight scenes, dropping ten minutes from the running time. It may seem strange to change such successful shows but these changes were proven correct by later audience response to the content and by the added satisfaction the cast got from performances with the new structures. For untrained actors especially, this ongoing analysis is a great help in keeping the work dynamic.

PROJECT STRUCTURE

Each project has physical limitations — the size of the group: time available for the overall project and for each session; space available for workshops and for performances; support materials available. Space and support materials are easy limitations to adapt to. The size of the group will affect the style. With a big group, broad strokes may be necessary, especially early in the project. Innovative delegation of tasks and leadership roles will help. If the class size is large then get lots of ideas listed and work on the large-group scenes first so that the group adopts habits of co-operation and discipline before you go on to more focused work.

Time is the major factor in structuring the work patterns. Too much can be as bad as too little. If you have the luxury of being able to take as long as you like to create the play, then I would strongly suggest that you set a definite performance date during the first few sessions so that you do have a goal and a sense of purposeful progress. At Shopfront I have created major plays in twelve once-a-week sessions of two and a half hours each, but that is difficult. In some school situations I have had the chance to work seven forty-minute periods per week for three weeks and that was also hard but possible. Shorter sessions are fine if they happen often, but if you are only working once a week you need a decent length of workshop session because so much time is needed in the re-capping process. With very advanced groups I have worked on shows all day — six to seven hours — five days a week. With shows for major touring we have worked all day once a week for eight months to create two plays, each about forty-five minutes long.

So there is no ideal time period for a project. You never seem to have enough rehearsal time at the end, so err on the generous side if you have the choice. Once the full time period is established it can be useful to divide it in three and allocate each third to a particular stage of the project. The first third

The Playground Play. Shopfront T.I.E. team. (Also televised by A.B.C.)

would be devoted almost wholly to new ideas and creating as many scenes and finding as much material as possible. There would be little emphasis at this time on structuring the play, though some scenes may be joined up opportunistically. You may also find that a good first scene and a good last scene are created but be sure to keep them tentative so that no scene possibilities are curtailed yet.

In the second third of the project, emphasis will be placed on the development of each scene, including songs, dance and other elements of the play. Performance direction will occur quite often and a positive search will be under way for linking devices. In this period the overall style of the show will be decided. Physical needs such as props, costumes, lights, sets, etc. will be decided upon also. The first and final scenes could be created now.

In the final third of the project the workshops should be moving strongly towards being full rehearsals. A lot of attention will be given to performance details and to developing rhythm, pacing and focus. The final structure of the play should be decided early in this period to give time for experiment and change. Final editing pressure must be applied too and harder questions can be asked now because the ideas are about to face audiences.

In the aftermath of performance it is also important to have a little period in which the group can discuss the success and shortcomings of the project and its impact on audiences.

Skeletons or Plans

Dealing with the many structural patterns that exist in a good playbuilding project demonstrates the complexity of the undertaking. The director must juggle and balance the many small 'skeletons' or structures which make up the overall project. The juggling must be dynamic, but controlled.

Developing a group feeling for structure is important. You must let the group sense that there is a compelling drive in the work, that there is an overall plan of development and that there is a strong logic to the many elements which will draw it all together into a real play. Early in the project you must point out structural elements in the work — show them the bones. It is difficult otherwise for young people to keep a grip on their belief in an end-product. Making them aware of structure eventually puts the structure into their hands.

To do all this the director needs to be something of a performer and must have a performer's feel for rhythm and control. You must try to conduct each workshop as the conductor of an orchestra would, moving each session through the individual passages and the group creations to a satisfying finale. All should have a sense of inevitable progress about it. This is achieved through the usual techniques of good teaching and good directing: through constantly affirming the interest, value and excitement of what the group is creating. Affirm all behaviour that progresses the creation and development of the play; clearly condemn behaviour that damages progress. All this is judged on the group's need to create the play, not on your idiosyncratic rules as a teacher or a director. This brings a sense of inevitable progress and of sure structuring towards the goal.

Drift and Catch

Achieving this inevitable sense of progress and structure is a matter of personal style. In early projects you may like to plot certain dates to check progress and then adapt the workshops to meet those goals. I mostly do this by feeling now, by trying to stay alert to the needs and moods of a group.

You can sense when a group may be feeling a little unsteady with their play and may want to take a session a bit more carefully. You can sense when a group is keen to work very hard and you must go with that surge. I often use a drifting structure — which I call Drift and Catch — and it is very useful at times. It is a little like allowing the improvisations to flow. You can let a workshop drift, amble about, lope along easily without obvious pressure and then when the group is about to drift away, you catch them and make them aware of the need to control the slide, make them aware of how they are losing direction and structure and what that means for the play. The moment when you 'catch' them must be used as a positive moment that can be learnt from and built upon.

The Workshop

Each workshop — after the first — can begin by going over the work already created and end by repeating the new work created in that session, with the final minutes being a repeat of their favourite scene. This is a fairly stock but useful structure to the workshop and is particularly good for new playbuilders. With a more experienced group you can afford to go faster and harder and with less fear of mistakes because a mistake means less to an experienced group.

Given that we have at least one scene created in the first workshop, the full pattern of a workshop, at each stage of the full time period for the project, might be illustrated as in the table on p.56.

This pattern may have to be adapted according to how much time you have for each session. Do try to have a variety of work in each workshop. Sometimes you may abandon the pattern to give a whole session over to a troublesome scene or to specific skills scenes, such as singing or dancing. Such a change of pattern can help emphasise the work nature of the project and emphasise the quality of work you are expecting them to achieve. And when the problem is solved or some real progress is perceived, that achievement gives more drive to the group and the project.

Structuring each scene

The scene is the basic building block of the play. The way in which you structure each scene will determine the overall strength of the play and will set a precedent for the way workshops and the

General Workshop Pattern	First Third of Project Time	Second Third of Project Time	Final Third of Project Time
1. Run through the scenes you already have.	1–2. Draw comments on development of ideas.	1–2. Draw comments on ideas, performances and on how to link scenes.	1–5. Emphasise structuring of play and rehearsal. Fine-tuning of ideas. Polish links between scenes. Sharpen focus points.
2. Discuss the scenes. 3. Discuss any material brought in by the group.	3. Bring material yourself for example and for discussion but not inclusion.	3. Rigorous testing of found material. Shape it to fit play.	
4. Read through notes about scene ideas and choose which to work on. 5. Create new scenes; discuss them; re-work them.	4–5. Simply create and collect scenes, unless obvious links suggest themselves.	4–5. Develop scenes fully and discuss linking them into a full play.	
6. Discuss practical aspects of the project.	6. Exact performance dates, places and times decided on.	6. Poster, program, props, costumes, discussed.	6. Finalise all business aspects — poster; front-of-house arrangements; program; backstage arrangements.
7. Re-play the scenes created in this session or those that need work.	7. Re-play to edit and to develop.	7. Develop scenes and links between scenes. Re-play with links. Discuss rhythm and pace and focus.	7. Should be full run-through if possible. If not, be sure to re-play at least 3 or 4 scenes in running order so that links are effectively rehearsed. Work on rhythm and pace.
(If a workshop does not allow time for full re-playing of scenes, it can be effective to talk through the scene ideas quickly.)			
8. Re-play the group's favourite scene or song.	8. Let them leave the workshop session with a real glow of achievement.	8. Let them leave the workshop session with a real glow of achievement.	8. Let them leave the workshop session with a real glow of achievement.

whole play will be handled. I take a scene to be any separate entity within the play and it can be a poem, song, dance, skills demonstration, dramatic scene, etc. While they are varied in their style and content, the scenes will usually have much the same backbone structure: beginning, climax, resolution. None of these terms need carry their full implications in every scene. The climax in some scenes may be quite gentle and in others outrageous. The resolution may be a complete tying off of ideas or may be a simple summation that leads to more questions. However, the strength of episodic plays lies very much in the consistent structural strengths of the individual scenes.

When dealing with a Story Play in which a structure will have been developed quite early in the project, the director should keep reminding the group of the overall pattern as they create the individual scenes. Groups can sometimes feel dissatisfied with the scenes in a story-line play if they do not retain that view of the larger plot. It can seem that a scene has not achieved anything if there is no finish to it; but in a Story Play tightly sealed scenes can give a jerky, erratic flow to the final play. It can be useful to have a large sheet of paper pinned up with the play skeleton on it so that the group can see at all times which piece of the work they are preparing.

With a Theme Play there is usually a lot of satisfaction achieved with each scene because they are complete within themselves, as well as contributing to a grander whole. The hard part, of course, comes when you try to put all those finished bits together into a dramatically satisfying structure called a play. That task is helped a great deal if each scene has been given clear structural attention. If the group is used to creating and discussing structure for these smaller elements, the job of structuring the play is less daunting.

Encouraging a very simple scene structure can be a great advantage. The kids can understand what you are talking about and the emphasis remains on the ideas rather than dramatic devices. A simple structure can be developed into a more sophisticated form but a complex structure will often distort the ideas and the performance capabilities of the group. As with almost everything in playbuilding, simplicity is the best base for building on. So I will usually suggest that the kids state very clearly at the beginning of a scene what the scene is about. Give the audience the information they need to understand what you are doing and who you are. Then expand that until you come to the main point of the scene. Then hit them with the punchline and stop.

Such a simple structure still carries within it the possibilities of great variety. But it also reminds the group of the basic requirements of their play — enough information for people to understand what's going on (or to be pleasantly puzzled); enough development to grasp the ideas the group want to put forward in this scene (including sheer fun or jokes); a satisfying conclusion. The editing and analysing process will help the group achieve good results in each of these areas.

Most of the discussion of these aspects of a scene should be taken from the audience point of view. If a scene has been running for some minutes — even for one minute — and the audience has not had information telling them who the people in the scene are and where they are (if those things are necessary), then you should be asking the kids these questions. 'Who is this person you're talking to? How will the audience know this person is your mother?' Remember that with an all-kid cast the audience does not have consistent physical clues as to characters and if the play is episodic one performer may be a mother in one scene, a baby in the next, a soldier in the next, a farmer in the next. The simple approach is usually the best — just tell the audience who you are. With a play based in plot, however, information given in earlier scenes need not be repeated.

If you call someone 'Mum' in a scene then the audience accepts that performer is the mum, even if the performer is a boy. In fact, this simple approach can solve casting problems as well. I have never had any real trouble getting boys to play female parts and girls to do male roles because I never ask them to act 'feminine' or 'masculine'. I do not ask for silly voices and butch or effeminate mannerisms, so the kids find it easy to be a member of the opposite sex, just as they can easily be older or younger. They simply say who they are and the audience will believe them.

Editing the beginning of a scene can also involve deleting unnecessary information. We may need to know that Irene is talking to Mum, but we probably do not need to know exactly where Mum is or what is on the TV right now, if the whole point of the scene is that Irene is arguing with Mum about her new boyfriend. As with many 'rules' in drama, the opposite rule can be just as true. The group may decide that if Mum tells the audience all about what she is watching on TV — pointless information — while Irene is trying to talk about something vital to her happiness, a dramatic contrast and a very emotional context is established. Whichever way the beginning goes, the purpose and the perceived effect of the material must be examined. What will an audience think if we do it this way; what if we do it that way?

The same examination must go into the climax. It can be useful to ask the group to pinpoint that peak in the scene and then to discuss how high the peak ought to be. Should Irene shout and scream at Mum until she gets attention and then storm out? Perhaps the peak can be when Mum misunderstands completely something Irene says and assumes she is commenting on the TV show that is the centre of Mum's world. A simple silence and a quiet exit, unnoticed by Mum, may then be an effective climax — and resolution.

Discussion of the scene development to its peak should involve several alternatives. As the director you should throw in some ideas even if you do not particularly believe in them. The discussion and then the decision to put a specific idea into place in the scene represents a very important process in the playbuilding work. No idea or scene should remain in place unchallenged. Sometimes a scene will be so right that everyone will yell with joy, 'That's it!' and you must be part of that joy and accept the absolute rightness of the scene. Then, three or four sessions later, you question that scene rigorously. Gaining re-affirmation of each idea and step in the playbuilding process develops deep understanding of the structure and firmer and firmer commitment to the work.

PUNCHLINES; EXITS; BLACKOUTS; CROSS-FADES; FREEZES

These are probably the most common ways to end scenes. Everyone will have personal preferences but you must be careful that your preference does not distort the purposes of the scenes and the play. My own great love is for punchlines but I have found on occasions that having too many scenes with great knockout endings created a play structure that was like a series of stand-up comic routines. This broke the strength of the play and created an effect of insincerity. The remedy was to change some of the endings.

Punchlines are most appropriate for episodic plays, especially Theme Plays. Freezes — tableaux — can be visual punchlines and can offer variety in scene endings. Punchlines tend to offer a twist in the tail of the scene whereas freezes offer an emphasis on some strong moment of the scene, leaving a lingering image for the audience to consider. I enjoy punchlines because they can be such dynamic manipulators of emotion and thought. Just when an audience is thinking in the expected manner, a good punchline can jolt them out of it.

One very poignant example of this was in a play created by a colleague. The scene was about incest, an issue that the cast had discussed at length and felt determined to make a serious statement about in their play on families. The scene was sincerely performed and very moving. The performers presented very difficult situations in a bold and honest manner. The scene showed several family situations in which incest was occurring and the cast performed these in small groups, each incident ending in a freeze. This concluded with five frozen moments of incest on view and one performer left whose job was to finish the scene. They tried various statements about the issue but these all seemed inadequate with the visual statements so strongly present. Another problem was that the scene had established a sombre mood that would be quite numbing to the audience and it was hard to top that or to say, well, let's just forget all this and go on with the rest of the play. But the play did have to go on. No-one wanted to change the scene itself because great thought and effort had gone into it and it made exactly the point they wanted to make.

I was called in to advise on the scene and the ending. To call in a sympathetic colleague is a useful thing to do when you are in a spot because he or she can often take a fresh and objective view. We tried several summing-up statements and fade-out exits, which did not work. I suggested that they use dramatic contrast to break the sombre spell and force the audience to snap out of their predictable thinking on the issue. In other words, tell a joke; put in a funny punchline. We devised a line — borrowed from somewhere — for the last performer to say. In the midst of the five tableaux of incest situations, the girl came forward and said, 'I never had incest with my family. They were too ugly.'

In performance this ending was explosive. Audiences laughed every time and then you could see them mentally kicking themselves for laughing. That laugh forced a re-think about the whole scene and about the serious points the performers were making. The use of the word 'ugly' at the end of the line and the scene carried connotations and reverberations that kept the scene echoing in the audience's minds for a long time. The stark contrast between the boldly honest scene and the black-joke punchline ensured a stronger audience impact than a simple, if horrific, presentation of facts could achieve.

The director must avoid imposing clever punchlines on the group. Suggest them, certainly, but you must allow the group to reject punchlines on simple grounds of 'doesn't feel right' or 'don't like it', no matter how clever and apt you think the line is.

My least favourite scene ending is a blackout. Blackouts can break up the flow of a play quite badly. I am not even keen on blackouts as an ending for a play. I usually have the cast exit to signal the end and only fade to black when they are almost offstage. I prefer the cast to create their own blackouts and fades. A freeze is a sort of blackout and so is an exit, but these have a human quality to them and a cast control component that a technical blackout lacks. I rarely use blackouts in the middle of a play, but prefer the cast to keep the action flowing with exit/entrance cross-fades. I emphasise that the cross-fade I mean here is one created by the performers, not by lighting changes. This keeps the timing and rhythms of the play securely in the hands of the cast and the human cross-fade is an effective scene ending, especially when a gentle ending is needed. The human cross-fade is also very important in Story, Character and Setting Plays.

The fade and cross-fade endings and beginnings of scenes must be carried out with precise timing. The idea of the cross-fade is that the new action begins just before the old action fades. You have to avoid those terrible moments when no-one is on stage; nothing is happening; dead spots. Scenes linked in this way help the performers during workshops to develop a finer sense of timing, pacing and rhythm to their work. The cross-fade gives an essential sense of continuity and unity to plays based in plot and also brings that sense to episodic plays. The cross-fade is a vital tool in preventing the episodic play from feeling too segmented and jerky in presentation.

Encourage and help the performers to manipulate their performance space for the best dramatic effect and benefit of the pacing of the play. With untrained actors it is always better to err on the side of pace rather than ask them to hold moments on stage that they have neither the skill nor inclination for. But there can be rewards in experimenting with the timing of exits and entrances because this work can help the group develop more dramatic control and more dramatic subtlety. It is also important that all entrances and exits have purpose to them; the idle drifting on and off of performers is detrimental to any play.

Exits do not have to take performers off the stage space. Quite often I have created plays where the performers stay on stage all the time. This can be very useful for development of discipline and concentration in the group and it also gives a feeling of the play being very much a group effort and statement. The performers in these cases create a performance territory on the stage area and establish boundaries that the audience accept.

This style of production also brings all the business of performance before the audience and that can provide a sense of openness and honesty. I have done shows where the cast sat at the back on the floor when not on stage or sat on chairs that formed a back wall to the performing territory, with their backs to the audience. In these cases the cast must be precise and business-like in all their off-stage actions. When facing the audience in an off-stage mode, I insist that the cast watch carefully the on-stage action, thus helping provide an even stronger focus on the action and avoiding distractions.

If this style of presentation is to be used, this should be decided fairly early in the workshops so that movement, especially entrances and exits, can be developed as the scenes are created. However, if a group is working well together, their off-stage activities will be easily transferable to in-sight presentation. The idea of all-on-stage performances can be discussed with each project so that a group has the chance to give their play the intensity that such a style can bring. I have found the all-on-stage style very useful with theatre-in-education shows where the performance is done in the school. It is very adaptable to any space because the cast actually define their own space — using a carpet square as your 'stage' can help — and the style brings a feeling of nothing-up-the-sleeves which school audiences appreciate.

FOCUS

In the early stages of scene development, focus requires little attention. But in the final third of the project it should become a vital element in the structure of a scene. Experiment with focus. Have the group move the focus from the central performer to a less significant point or person on the stage and then discuss the audience effect of this. Question the group often about where they want the focus to be in each scene. 'Where should the audience be looking now?' is my frequent question, and in my director mode I can comment on where I think I would be looking if I were the audience. Sometimes the answers are surprising and you should not be scared of having unusual focus points during the play. Having a focus on a little girl who is burying her dead budgerigar while her parents argue loudly over money can offer a strong moment. The loudest, brightest, most violent person on stage is not always the most important person. Ensuring a variety of focus situations — some blatant, some gentle — can enrich the response to the play.

It is important then that the group be aware of the need for structure at all times. If people see ways to link scenes as they are being created — even very early in the project — then that should be encouraged and those links should be maintained so they become integral to the group's understanding of the progress of the project.

In a play about performance — *Off-Key* — some Shopfront kids wanted to show how they had felt being pushed around by adults in auditions for movies and TV ads. One girl said she was always being told to calm down, not to be so lively. The scene that arose out of that had a very simple structure and made some interesting points about focus. The Girl walked onto the stage, a ball of energy with red hair and freckles, bright clothes and hand-painted sandshoes. Below her was an agent figure who told her to sing. The Girl sang a silly, bouncy song very energetically. Almost immediately the Agent started yelling at her, 'Stay in one spot!' 'Remember the cameras!' 'Don't dance!' The Girl was enjoying herself too much to pay attention to the Agent, who grabbed hammer and nails, and holding the Girl's feet, nailed both shoes to the stage. Then he stepped back and said, 'That's better,' as the Girl sang on for a line or two, moving her arms about wildly to try to give life to the song. The Girl bowed for applause and the Agent left as the audience clapped. The Girl bent down and held her shoes — the big nails looked as if they had gone through her feet as well — and stepped out of the shoes, leaving them nailed to the stage for the rest of the play. That image of the nailed-down shoes became central to the structure of the play, as well as an enjoyable visual punchline to the scene.

In this scene the beginning gave simple information by the respective positions, costumes and actions of the characters. The song was a distracting but fun element. Nailing down the shoes was the climax and made the major point of the scene. The nailing of the shoes certainly focused audience attention and made the later, lingering image of those shoes an effective motif. Stepping out of the shoes was the punchline; a nice twist in showing that kids can still walk away from these inhibiting situations. A cross-fade ending kept the point clean, clear and quick. The ongoing shoes image linked the scene into the overall theme and structure of the play.

SUMMARY

- Successful structuring of *each element* of the project will lead to a strong play and good performances.
- You must also structure your relationship with the group, erasing yourself as the project progresses. The play must belong to the group, not to the director. You should not need to be present at performances.
- Have a final assessment session after the performances. Continue to make needed changes if performances continue.
- Structure project development to meet limitations of group size, time, space and material available.

- When time-frame is established, divide project into three periods:
  1) Create ideas and scenes;
  2) Develop scenes fully; link some scenes; find first and final scenes;
  3) Structure whole play; refine and rehearse; attend to business aspects.
- Be a conductor of workshops; use rhythm and control. Affirm creative behaviour; condemn behaviour that harms progress towards the play.
- Structure workshops in response to moods and needs of the group. Let workshops drift at times but catch them when structure is about to be lost.
- *Workshop structure* — Maintain clear pattern of work. Begin and finish with the accumulated scenes. End on a re-play of their favourite scene.
- *Scene structure* — Keep it simple; add complexity once strong skeleton is there. Backbone is: beginning; climax; resolution.
- *Episodic or Theme Play* — Each scene will have its own, satisfying structure. The play will finally have many dramatic peaks and scene endings. These moments must be structured into a dramatically satisfying pattern.
- *Story Play* — Remind group of the overall plot structure and where each scene fits, as scenes are developed.
- Begin each scene by giving audience the information they need to understand the scene.
- *Climax* — Discuss and try alternatives so an accurate decision is achieved. No idea or scene should remain in place unchallenged.
- *Resolution* — Experiment to ensure the scene ending is dramatically satisfying. Don't settle for the obvious.
- *Punchlines* suit episodic plays. Freezes (tableaux) are visual punchlines.
- *Blackouts* — Avoid them; they represent mechanical control.
- *Cross-fades* — Created by the performers — *not* by lighting change — these have great advantages. Cross-fades keep timing and rhythm in the hands of the cast. They are very important in Story, Character and Setting Plays.
- *Exits and entrances* must be controlled and timed precisely. These teach performers about manipulating their space.
- *All-cast-on-stage shows* can help performers develop discipline and concentration and offer audiences an intense and honest presentation.
- *Focus* — Experiment. Ask, 'Where should the audience be looking right now?'

THE PLAYGROUND PLAY

This play was really three projects, resulting in three different plays that were all based on the scenario created for the first production. There were sixteen young people in the first production, mixed in ages from ten to eighteen. This was Shopfront's first production and was created for performance in a children's playground at a Pre-School Centre. The playground had a small wooden cottage and we used the verandah as a stage while the audience sat outside in the playground. We performed in the sandpit and on the slippery-dip; inside and outside a window into a room of the cottage; around the outside of the low wire fence that enclosed the playground. There were two trampolines outside the fence which we used in a family argument scene. The play was presented at sunset and lights were used for the final scenes when it was almost dark.

The play developed as a rather strident statement of children's rights and used material from the work of John Holt, as well as quotes from Blake, Shakespeare and nursery rhymes. In the first production I imposed a number of modern songs and a piece of Beethoven's Ninth as introduction to the play, with the Ninth repeated in the climactic scene. One boy in the group played the tuba and we used his tuba as a way of attracting attention. This boy developed into an Outsider who did lots of outrageous things to try to gain his parents' love.

The production had a strong effect on parents, most of whom were seeing their kids speak out for the first time. Many commented that they really enjoyed the play but did not like what it said. This is a great power of playbuilding which can enable a group to develop an entertaining play even though its messages may be hard for its audiences to accept. ABC Radio made a special program about this project. When Shopfront got its own premises the kids wanted to do *The Playground Play* as the first full production there. I insisted that we have a new cast so that the play would be re-worked. We called it *The Playground Re-play*, and it had a cast of ten, mixed in age from twelve to seventeen. It was performed indoors so many of the scenes had to be staged differently, but we kept the staging very simple, using a carpet as main space and some raised platforms. By now I had realised that the taped music had to go but the cast insisted on retaining Beethoven's Ninth which had a predictable impact on the audience and was appropriate to two dramatic moments in the play.

This production had a powerful effect on both kids and parents. We held discussions with the audience after each show. After a season at Shopfront, it went to an international education conference in Adelaide.

The third production, the scenario of which appears below, was developed for the Shopfront Theatre-in-Education team for performances in High Schools. It had a cast of five, all aged sixteen or seventeen. They were the youngest team ever given approval by the Education Department to perform in schools and they toured around NSW for eight months with the show. The play had to be adapted for the small cast but the major issues and many scenes remained. ABC Television made a special program for the Year of the Child and this was shown nationally.

It is fair to say that these plays set out to be provocative and they sparked many strong discussions. When a playbuilt show deals with a touchy issue, it seems to me important that audience members should have the chance to discuss it with the cast and the director and that this requirement should be built into the project early in the process. The group is then brought to realise that their views may provoke argument and need to be defended and discussed. As issues must be discussed critically and at length during a playbuilt project, the kids usually become quite adept at putting their ideas forward. Audience discussions are testing situations and the group will need the support of the playbuilding director at these times.

Many of the scenes were created from the personal experiences of the kids. Ideas that — at the time — seemed radical were also seen to be supported by the poems of William Blake, for example. Some of the ideas have since become accepted in a society that is now more willing to examine through the mass media issues of abuse against children and of rights for young people. I think it is important that playbuilding projects offer their participants the chance to develop ideas and attitudes beyond their usual range; it is an educational tool as well as an entertainment. But because playbuilding also offers a very emotional working environment, it is vital that the director counter that pressure with rational and precise discussion on issues. Clarity of thought mixed with the emotional energy of creating theatre offers a dynamic learning and teaching process.

With this production the play did not end with the performance. The discussion became part of the play. Discussion is an important aspect of a production for schools, but this was not the only reason for deciding on this ending. When in the Re-Play at Shopfront the Rebel lying dead in the Outsider's arms raised his head and said, 'Look at me, Mum. I'm dead,' the impact was enormous; but some people felt that the level of emotional manipulation was dishonest. The play's argument was deliberately one-sided and the casts had always been prepared to discuss that with audiences. But the T.I.E. cast decided that it would be unfair to compel audiences in schools to applaud a play that many, if not most, would disagree with. That could alienate those who were at least prepared to think about the issues. This matter was discussed at great length and all the team were concerned to avoid applause and to offer a more objective ending, achieved with our Brechtian presentation of an emotional ending. These decisions made the production a very effective project for schools and the discussion after the shows was always lively and always right on the issues.

(Note: The detailed description and quotes here come from the script of *The Playground Play* which was prepared by the T.I.E. cast for the A.B.C. Television production of the play. The script is published through Shopfront Theatre.)

Scenario for THE PLAYGROUND PLAY

Theatre-in-Education version. Cast: David Cummings; Jason Dann; Bridget Dwyer; Beverley Jay; Ken Russo.

The set is a carpet square when possible. Usually, it is a set of chairs at the back; some face the audience and some face away, forming an offstage area. Props are on the floor, under the chairs.

PLAYTIME — The cast are seated with backs to audience. One plays 'Song of Joy' on a recorder. Mum stands and announces, 'Time to play!' The Kids play as Mum walks up and down, using a battery megaphone, declaring slogans at them. 'Money doesn't grow on trees. Act your age. Don't play with yourself. Boys don't cry. Don't talk to strangers.' And many more. The Kids repeat the slogans joyfully, showing off how well they have learned. Jason, the Outsider, stutters as he tries to say the slogans. They laugh at him. Mum encourages each Kid in playing with toys that indicate what they will grow up to be: war-toys for Ken; Bridget will be a teacher or nurse and a mummy; David will be a brave fireman. Jason doesn't know what he wants to be so they laugh at him.

CHILD MOLESTATION — Bridget is easily tricked by a man in dark glasses into going off with him. As they leave, two Researchers announce statistics and facts about child abuse. Mum counters with new slogans 'Don't talk to people you know. ' The Researchers sing a parody of a Sesame Street song 'A child molester is a person in your neighbourhood' — and the facts are presented in bright, breezy fashion. Bridget even asks, 'What if the kid likes it?' Mum says, 'You'll go to hell.' The scene ends with the Molester smiling at the audience, putting his arm around Bridget and walking away with her. In a cross-fade, Bev comes forward and begins reciting her poem.

'THE NURSES SONG', BY WILLIAM BLAKE — Recited by Bev. (Each cast member had found or selected a poem on the play's themes and each poem was presented in the same way, from memory and out front, direct to the audience. This poem was in all three

BETTER   versions of the play, and is from 'Songs of Experience'. It deals with the theme of repression of adolescent sexuality.

BETTER   A series of boastful statements. 'I'm stronger than you' 'I'm prettier than you. ' The statements become bizarre so that everything can be boasted about. Delivery is very rapid. 'I have less friends than you'. 'I came first'. 'I came last'. Possessions are boasted about, and parents. 'My dad's a policeman'. 'My dad's a crook'. 'My mum's a doctor'. 'My mum's dead'. The scene ends in chanting about being the best. Some sit on the chairs and when the chanting finishes, they become an ordinary family, suddenly realistic in performance.

MUM   The time when Dad comes home; Mum is trying to get help in the kitchen. Bridget is a dole bludger; Jason is on the phone non-stop; David is a child who wants attention all the time. Mum tries to transfer some of the pressure to Dad who just wants peace. Mum rushes off hysterically and all becomes calm; everyone stops playing the games they were using against Mum. David and Dad do a crossword and the scene ends on a gentle punchline: 'A childbearer in three letters?' 'Mum, of course.' 'Let's do the next one.'

ALL ALONE   Jason tells how nobody loves him and he must be horrible. As he repeats this, the others come to him and hug him, tell him he's great, etc. He is invited to a party but says no. He walks off saying, 'I'm all alone. Nobody loves me.'

'CAREFULLY TAUGHT', BY RODGERS AND HAMMERSTEIN   As Jason walks off, the others applaud and David walks forward, hands clasped, and sings this song as if he is a small boy. (This scene was added by the T.I.E. cast.) The song says that hate and fear and prejudice are taught to people, mostly by their families. At the end, Bridget says, 'Isn't he cute?'

GOOD FAMILY   Robert runs to Mum and tells what a good boy he was at kindergarten. All the family members tell of their wonderful lives in grossly exaggerated 'happy' style. Each has a set speech that they keep repeating to all other members of the family. (Mum: 'I had a really busy day today. I went outside and did the washing, I cleaned the venetians and did all the ironing. Being a housewife and mother sure is rewarding.') The Twins are hugely successful at school and Dad is a banker who saves pensioners from having their mortgages foreclosed. They are all breathless with joy. Robert is going to run away from home because they're having apple pie and he doesn't like it. But he changes his mind and they all smile into the audience for a frozen 'happy' moment. Then the others walk off, leaving Jason behind, as he starts to recite his poem.

(Note: This scene and the 'Bad Family' scene were borrowed by the cast of *The Playground Re-Play* from *The Twins versus General Injustice*. Some of them had seen that play and thought these scenes, made shorter and more stylised, expressed the ideas better than the family scenes in the first *Playground Play*.

Names: In this scene the child was called Robert as a tribute to the person who created the scenes in the 'Re-Play'. Usually I encourage playbuilders to use their own names in the play as this emphasises that the ideas are theirs. It is also easier in a multi-scene play for the performers to remember the cast names than numerous names of 'characters'.)

'INFANT SORROW', BY WILLIAM BLAKE   Recited by Jason. Theme — the unwilling surrender of the infant to adult control. Included in all versions of the play. As Jason walked back to the chairs, two of the others came forward singing to begin the next scene.

ADVERTS	Based mostly around the McDonald's ads, this scene emphasises the sexual connotations in much advertising aimed at teenagers. At the end the cast, in provocative poses, sing, 'We've got it all. To go!' They freeze.
BAD FAMILY	As the freeze breaks up, Mum asks, 'Hi Robert, how was kindergarten?' The scene then proceeds with exactly the same style and overly energetic 'happiness' as in the 'Good Family' scene. But this time Robert has burnt down the kindergarten; the Twins have raped their teachers; Mum has bedded all the tradesmen who called; and Dad foreclosed on ten pensioners. Robert says he is leaving home because he is never included in the incest and the others tell him to go. As they walk away Ken comes forward and says his poem.
'A POEM FOR PARENTS', BY KHALIL GIBRAN	Recited by Ken. (Note: This poem was found and added by this cast who were asked to bring in found material as with the earlier two casts.) The poem says that children are their own selves, not the possessions of their parents.
I'M PREGNANT	As Ken finishes, Jason starts yelling for attention, telling Mum that he is pregnant. 'You thought I didn't know anything about sex, just 'cause you wouldn't tell me.' Then he realises that it's Mary who is pregnant and that he is totally confused. When he stops, Mum comes and takes his hand and says, 'Now, Jason dear, it's time you learnt about life.'
LIFE	Mum introduces Jason to the 'professional' people who will look after him all his life so he needn't think about anything. The people are Doctor, Lawyer, Teacher, Politician and Boss, who each make a speech. (The speeches were created and refined from the rather cynical views all three casts had towards these positions.) Mum finishes by reeling off a few more slogans for him. As she finishes the others step down from the chairs that they have been pontificating from and break into dance/movement as they sing the next scene.
'HELLO 12', BY KLEBAN AND HAMLISCH	This song from *A Chorus Line* — a very brief version — was added by the T.I.E. cast. It tells of the doubts as love and sex raise their bothersome heads in the teen years.
ROMEO AND JULIET	Using the megaphone, David calls for people to step up for the 'true love auditions'. Each pair does a short passage from the balcony scene in *Romeo and Juliet*. As each pair gets into the scene, David declares that this is filth and shoots the actors. The scene is done between two girls first, then a girl and boy, then two boys. David is disgusted each time and ends the scene by saying, 'All teenagers ever think about today is sex!' Bev stands and says her poem. (Note: The *Romeo and Juliet* scene was longer in the first version of this play. The kids used the window of the cottage as the balcony and the wooer on the ground would climb into the room and embrace the Juliet, only to be shot. The shootings inside the room were rather more frightening.)
'THE GARDEN OF LOVE' BY WILLIAM BLAKE	Recited by Bev. In all three versions. On the theme of repression of love and sexuality in youth.
IGNORED	This family scene had begun to form on the chairs behind Bev as she recited her poem. Ken is the adored child; Bridget is ignored. She tries telling more and more outrageous stories to attract attention but to no avail. Finally, they do hear her when she says she is going out on Saturday night. Dad gives her a lecture on all the dangers, saying she can't go, and ends with, 'The only time you ever speak to your family is when you want something'.
STREAKER	Jason, as the Outsider, yells that he is going to be a streaker. 'Look at me,

mum! I'm going to take off all my clothes!' The others treat this as a joke. Jason strips to his jeans and as he unzips them the others rush forward. Bev covers his crutch with her Cleo magazine which falls open to reveal a near-nude, male centre-fold. They rush Jason back to the chairs.

SCHOOL A whistle blast closes off the last scene and introduces this one. Jason is getting dressed and Mum tells him how he will enjoy his first day at school. Each segment of this scene begins and ends with a sharp blast on the whistle. Jason questions the use of what he is taught at school. He wants to be a poet. Dad says, 'Poetry doesn't put bread on the table'. The use of exams is questioned. (All these pieces are very brief with broad arguments for and against being declared. But the emotional tone is anti-school and opposed to the conformity the scene's creators declared came from schooling.) Definitions of school subjects in cynical manner. The report card. Lines from William Blake: 'To see a world in a grain of sand, And a heaven in a wild flower,' etc. Sexist teacher argues with the girls. 'Smart alecs are only boys' they tell him. Angry teacher who humiliates all the students: 'Without school you'd be savages. ' Jason is rejected by the other students for asking stupid questions and trying to be different: 'Leave us alone and let us get on with learning'. Jason explains how he wants to be a poet but at school he must sit in a room when the sun is out and wear shoes and make his poems rhyme: 'Everywhere they're afraid — afraid of questions, afraid of emotions, afraid of colour and poetry'. As he speaks, Song of Joy is played softly on the recorder. He finally declares: 'That's what all our lessons are — fear!' He goes to the back and shoots him-self.

(Note: This last speech was written by me and edited by each cast. It was based on a poem brought in by one of the original cast members. That poem was written by a boy who wanted to be a painter and felt so constrained at school that he committed suicide. Most of the images came from the poem.)

JOHN HOLT Based on ideas in John Holt's book, *Escape From Childhood*. Ken stands on a chair, brandishing John Holt's book. He quotes from the book, putting forward kids' rights arguments — the right to vote; to work for money; to travel; to privacy; to choose where to live and who to live with; 'the right to do in general what any adult may legally do.' The others try to shout him down. They tell him that protesting is out of date. Ken says, 'When we have a society where everyone is free and equal, then protesting will be old-fashioned. Idealism will never be out of date.' There is a brief freeze and then all the cast move towards the audience, speaking urgently as they move.

REVOLUTION Each cast member moves into a different section of the audience and preaches revolution. The speech made by each cast member is the same but not spoken in unison. It is a call to join them to fight for kids' rights. They ask who is ready to join them and plead for more volunteers. The speeches end with the cast declaring, 'We need action now!' They all shout, 'Now! Now! Now! Now!' Bridget stands on a chair and begins the chant of 'Power to kids!' which all the others join in very loudly. (None of this relies on audience participation.) After several chants, the cast freeze with fists clenched and held high.

THE END Jason comes forward and explains that he was in this play before and describes how it used to end. As he describes the actions, the cast carry them out. Mum shoots the Rebel, Bridget. (In the first production, the Rebel stood on top of the slippery-dip and when she was shot she slid down it into the arms of the other kids who then carried her into the cottage.) Mum then calls, 'Time for dinner, kids'. She offers bribes of chocolate pudding and presents and a good movie on TV. The kids go in for dinner and sing, 'Baa baa black sheep' as they go. (In the first production the kids went into the cottage and pressed their faces to the window as they sang, looking out at the sunset.) Then Jason kneels down beside the Rebel and says, 'Look at me, mum. I'm dead.' (In the *Re-Play* the lights in the theatre would then slowly fade.) Then Jason explains that they don't do the ending like that any more because some people felt the ending meant that kids wanted to destroy things like school and family. Bev says, 'But we don't. We just want things that are bad to change'. The cast each bring a chair forward, close to the audience, as they make some suggestions about other ways of doing things. Ken says, 'There are a lot of alternative family and school set-ups now. They don't all work. But the families and schools most people have don't work for a lot of people. Look at the divorce rate. Look at the amount of child bashing'. Jason says, 'There have to be better ways.' Bev says, 'What do you think?' Then the cast becomes involved with direct discussion with the audience.

CHAPTER 6

STRUCTURING 2
THE WHOLE PLAY

Many people find the structuring of a playbuilt show the most difficult job in the process, especially with a Theme Play. However, a lot of the structure will come from practical necessity and much of it will be implicit in the material created. It is important to allow the material to shape the play as much as possible. The final structure must not be forced. It must fit the needs of performers and material and feel as if the play grew naturally into its final shape. A number of different structures may suit your play; you only have to find one of them. Try to develop the structure that propels the drama of the material.

These points require discussion and apply to all types of playbuilt plays. Even with a Story Play a lot of attention must be given to the dramatic structure of the play. Not all Story Plays tell their stories in a simple fashion, in straight time sequence. Sometimes it is more useful to begin a story at the end and then use the drama to show how that final situation came about. A Character Play may save its most dramatic revelations for the end, or may have equally valid dramatic reasons to reveal the most astonishing things first. A Setting Play may need to reveal at the start a dramatic reason for focussing attention on this place.

A strong grasp on the purpose behind the play — what it is trying to say — is essential when discussion about the play's structure begins. And there must be discussion. Even if the whole group feels that they have found a simple and satisfying structure while developing the play, there can be a danger in accepting the easiest and most obvious solution. Persuade the group to try a number of shapes for their play, if possible, so that the final decision is truly a considered one.

Structuring a Story or Character Play where a narrative is the basic skeleton is, in many ways, more difficult than structuring an episodic play because much of the work must be done while the play is being built. In these cases, you should have a draft structure developed in the first few workshops. Many of the comments below about varying the scenes, offering echoes, using patterns, taking note of practical needs, etc. must be taken into account while in the process of building any play so that a good mixture of material is available for the final structure. But in the case of a narrative, plot-based play structural needs for the whole play will assume equal importance with scene structuring all through the process.

PRACTICAL NEEDS

Quite often a play will structure itself on practical grounds. By the time you get to deciding the final structure you will have a list of the scenes, songs and poems that have been created. This list will have the titles the group has given to each episode 'Ignored', 'Infant Sorrow', 'Mum', etc, and you should add to this the names of the performers in each. That list in itself will decide a lot of the structure. For example, in *The Twins versus General Injustice*, costumes had been devised for the TV-set characters. Therefore a scene without those actors had to be placed before the Live Show scene to give time for the actors to change costume. The sheer awkwardness of getting a particular grouping onto the performance area can dictate when their scene occurs. You may decide to bring them on after a solo scene which would also offer a contrast in complexity and cast size between the two scenes.

Avoid awkward linking of scenes, especially physically awkward links. If a group or a prop has to be manoeuvred onto the stage, cover it with a scene out front that will hold the audience's attention. The dramatic flow can be lost if the audience is just watching people on a stage struggling with set changes or trying to cope with awkward stage-traffic patterns. No-one objects to being able to see the stage business occurring, as long as it is done efficiently and they have something of substance to involve them while the mechanics occur. In these linkages, as in so much else in theatre, timing and efficiency are all, rather than artistry. Good structure will ensure that the cast are able to do the jobs required in the play. The ability of the cast to carry out the business of the play is just as important to a successful show as any performance skill. A group of kids may not be good actors but they should all be good workers.

The structure of a play must be practical. It must help the cast get on with their work. It must support the most plodding person in the play. The bright, bouncy ones will not need so much help, but a good structure will provide a framework from which to launch their energies. The structure should give the cast confidence in their play and in their own abilities. The cast must understand the structure. They should understand the emotional, intellectual and dramatic patterns formed by the structure. The better they understand the structure, its purposes and effects, the better they can perform their jobs.

BALANCE

The structure of a play should have balance, harmony, aptness. This does not necessarily mean symmetry because an ugly or misshapen form may reflect perfectly the subject matter. The final shape has to feel right to the director and the cast. That takes a lot of analysis at times. The structure is the last chance to make the play really wonderful, so it must never be acceptable to say, 'It'll do', about the structure. The sense of balance I refer to is very difficult to define because of the many variables in a play and a performance. The shape must balance with the content; must dress and present the content to its best effect. The shape must balance with the cast and present their efforts to best effect.

In *S.K.Y.* the shape of the play reflected the uncomplicated story and attitudes of the group. The simplicity of the links kept the group's efforts concentrated on the story and helped a large group, of very mixed abilities, carry out their jobs. Because the story was propelled by the structure, audiences were held. Because the very direct story-line held, the humorous scenes worked well. The talented performers were able to soar in their 'spots', confident that the structure would hold behind them and that the diversionary performance moments would not weaken the framework. The boomerang effect of the last scene returning to the first provided a nice balance of action and meaning.

The problems of achieving a balanced structure for a play are similar to those of any artistic construction. I would compare it with constructing a poem because so much importance is placed on rhythm and imagery. Like a poem, a play can be lyrical or narrative; it can rhyme or be blank verse; its

Coffee shop scene from *Love Matters*.

images may be symbolic, decorative or harshly real; and its rhythms may be jarring or flowing, relentless or gentle. Learning to balance these poetic elements with the practical demands of movement, staging, content and cast is the hardest job of the director and one that is best learnt from experience. These notes can only be limited indicators of the many possibilities.

Bringing a poetic sensibility to the task helps, but you also need the eye of the painter, the ear of the musician, a feel for the rhythms of movement and speech, the sense of timing needed by a good film editor, the objectivity of an academic, the practicality of a carpenter, and a strong commitment to your group. If you can manage to remain deeply humble at the same time, you are well on the way to being able to construct a play perfectly!

Balancing the shape of a play is similar to patterning the play but may be a little more obvious or practical. If you have two songs in a play you will usually place them in balance within the structure, perhaps one three scenes in and the other three scenes from the end. Scenes that echo each other should be spaced so a feeling of balance is achieved. Monologues and poems may be spaced for balance too. In *The Playground Play*, the 'Good Family' and the 'Bad Family' scenes were identical in style and almost so in content. The dialogue of both was deliberately repetitious to imprint the ideas in the audience's minds. If the joke of the 'Bad Family' was to work effectively it had to be close enough to 'Good Family' for the audience to remember but not so close that it seemed unsubtle. When we placed a brief but powerful poem in between the two scenes the gap was too small and the poem was squashed. We put the poem and a contrasting humorous scene together and they formed a good buffer between the 'Family' scenes. This segment of four scenes created a little shape of its own within the play and held a satisfying strength because of that.

Balance in the shape of a play can be a dramatically pleasing quality. I sometimes draw myself a little shape in which to fit the scenes. A megaphone shape will start soft/small and grow and grow to loud/large — or use the reverse-megaphone shape. One of my favourites is the hour-glass shape which brings the play into an intense centre from a large, maybe generalised, beginning and then opens out again to an expansive ending. In the play, *Replica*, the shape of a game of Monopoly was used and a floor design of the Monopoly board emphasised that structure. The circular play ends where it began. The linear play follows a straight line and is usually narrative. This idea of shapes may be useful for you and your group to help you visualise the overall structure of the play.

The idea of visualised shapes reminds me of a game you could buy when I was a kid. It was a three-dimensional jigsaw and each of these shapes was quite attractive in itself. When put into the right combination, the different shapes would all slot so tightly together that you could not tell where one began and the other ended, and together they formed a new and interesting shape. That is my idea of the perfect structure for a play.

RUNNING TIME

The running length of any play is a practical issue. On your list of scenes it is useful to have a note of the running time of each scene in performance. That element can be very important in ordering the scenes. A certain rhythm to the play is established immediately from the length of each scene. You can speed up a section by bunching short scenes together; two or three long scenes together can give a sense of seriousness and substance. An audience's involvement in a play can be manipulated by the rhythms set up by scene lengths.

In *The Twins versus General Injustice*, the workshops had produced a lot of ideas that were short and punchy, making their points like jokes. When we came to structure the play we realised that this mass of quick scenes would make the play fractured. We decided to package a number of the short scenes together and give them a structure of their own by introducing a narrator who explained the story of 'The Seven Deadly Social Diseases'. That gave this new 'scene' a unity and a beginning, middle and end that felt satisfying.

The other bunch of scenes also had a common theme to do with liberation issues. We developed very rapid links between them all and used protest signs as a motif. The speed with which the short scenes were done was the most vital element because each small piece was virtually a beginning and an end with no middle; each was a set-up that ended in the sharp twist of a punchline. This rapid-fire delivery provided an almost continual laughter/shock reaction to what was now a single scene, labelled for ourselves as, 'Protest Movements.' We followed this fragmented sequence with a static, talky scene that changed the pace completely.

The length of the piece and the allocation of time within it are issues to be looked at closely in the final editing. When several scenes are put together you will discover that the amount of time given to each may no longer seem satisfactory. A scene that runs three minutes in workshops may be fun and enjoyed by all yet appear too long when placed beside other scenes. You may find that content is repeated and seems better stated in other scenes, or maybe we have seen too much of a particular character or performer or issue. It is almost inevitable that placing a bunch of scenes into a structure will also affect the impact each scene now has. You may even find that some scenes need to be lengthened to provide more information.

With *Love Matters*, the play at the end of this chapter, our particular cast needs were that we were taking this play on tour and we wanted all twelve of the cast to have an almost equal share in the performance. When we came to the structuring of the play we found a real imbalance. Further scenes were created and some roles shifted around until we had a more even distribution of performance time and status for each cast member. This refinement could only have been made at that structuring stage. Up to that point the imbalance had not been clear to anyone.

CONTRAST

As in many aspects of playbuilding work, the use of contrast is invaluable when developing a final structure. Contrasts can be patterned on many different levels. A large cast scene followed by a monologue; a noisy scene followed by a quiet one; happy followed by sad; complex and simple

— there are many examples that can be given. When you look at your list of scenes, study it for contrasts.

Contrast is especially important in controlling the emotions of the audience. Making a joke at the most serious moment, or inserting a simple moment of seriousness into a humorous scene are both effective devices for controlling audience mood. This can be achieved by the juxtaposition of scenes as well. A common problem is created by directors when they stack too many serious scenes together to try to prove that their group really do have deep thoughts on the issues. Most young people, I find, are not very keen to be 'too serious'. They enjoy making serious points as long as there is humour as well. Take care to structure the play in keeping with the attitudes of the group.

Contrast can be provided in easy steps too. You may sometimes find the gap in mood between two scenes is too great to sustain audience commitment. In that case you may like to ease the audience from one situation to another. In *Piece by Piece*, we had a rather frightening scene near the end. It was called, 'If I Had A Gun . . .', and was a series of speeches about the capacity to kill. It followed an hilarious scene in which the cast taught the audience about the 'Australian Peace Plan'. Putting the very serious scene straight after it did not work at all. The shift in mood was too extreme. We decided to put a simple song in between the two scenes: a boy's statement about finding his own sense of peace. The simplicity and quietness of the song brought the audience back from the laughter, thus providing a gentler contrast and an easier transition into the more bleak scene.

REPEATING PATTERNS AND ECHOES

Repeating patterns of ideas, movement, visuals, groupings, scene beginnings and/or endings, music, slogans/phrases/catchcries, etc, can add a deep dramatic strength to the work. Repetition, carefully placed and designed, can give a reverberation to an entire play that will make it ring in the audience's minds for a long time. These echoes are like a hidden, sub-structure to the play. The more subtly placed the patterns are, the more intriguing and lingering the reverberation is.

The drama of an episodic play can be propelled effectively through the variation of repeated patterns. The repetition provides structural strength and the variation drives the drama. In *Dancing with Kangaroos*, the central dramatic issue, 'What do we think Australia is all about?', is contained, explained and presented almost entirely through the variation and repetition of the second scene. This scene, called 'Drysdale', was without dialogue and set up a number of characters who moved to and fro in a number of set patterns with clear indications of relationships between men and women, men and men, adults and children, and attitudes towards anyone 'different'.

The repetition scene was called 'Drysdale Exposition'. It repeated the earlier scene and then extended it to demonstrate some development of each character and the background to their actions. The scenes in between had illuminated many of the attitudes being exposed in these two scenes so that the extension of the 'Drysdale' scene made sense. The repetition and opening out of the scene gave power and clarity to the points the group wanted to make. The repeated pattern also gave the audience the satisfaction of feeling the play come to a dramatically logical conclusion. By the final scene this repetition had made the audience familiar with the territory under exploration — an important factor as the play was created mainly for overseas audiences. But even in Australia the repeated pattern was important in narrowing the range of argument and reinforcing for the audience the boundaries of the discussion.

Much of the work of planting the echoes and repeated patterns needs to be done in the scene creation stage. The director will try to pick up moments, events, themes, movements and characters that the group feels are significant. When opportunities arise, these 'iconic' moments can be threaded into other scenes. Look for possibilities of encouraging echoes, always explaining that these will arouse emotional and intellectual responses in the audience. There is a world of difference between bland repetition and echoes or repeated patterns. The difference lies in the emotional content. Good repetition should act like a musical motif.

VARIATIONS IN PATTERNS

I must emphasise that the elements of a play that can bear effective repetition and echoing have to be chosen carefully. Except when exact and precise repetition is the point you wish to make, you need to devise variations such as occur in music when a different tempo is used or a different instrument or combination of instruments re-plays the motif. Watch that the group does not fall back on comfortable patterns when creating scenes. If there is not an emotional frisson, or a good laugh, or some deliberate dramatic purpose, or an extra revelation connected to an echo or repeated pattern, then it is probably just a boring bit of repetition that will look lazy in the play. It is your job as director to prevent lazy repetition.

One of the most common repetitions to occur in playbuilding is the use of scenes with only two or three people involved. Some plays offer duologue after duologue because the director has not pushed to have more complex drama created by the group. It is true that a play *can* be structured to offer a dramatic balance of duologue scenes, deliberately created to make a point. In that case the purpose will be conveyed to the audience.

VISUAL STRUCTURE

As well as hearing the words and noting the actions of the play, an audience is very aware of visual patterns occurring on stage. A very effective framework can be created through such use. An economical use of props can also weave a pattern into a play. In *Dancing With Kangaroos* we used a bunch of sticks to represent a baby in the main scenes. This Baby was wrapped in a blanket which was allowed to unroll at appropriate moments and the sticks would clatter to the ground. The sticks were also used as wood for the barbecue and to create an iconic pattern representing the land. The dropping and picking up of the sticks occurred four times in the play. This play also used umbrellas in a number of different situations and ended with all characters holding umbrellas aloft. By the end of the play these umbrellas had gained a symbolic power not present in the first two or three scenes. Repeated use of the umbrellas in strongly dramatic situations provided a visual meaning that took on a power all its own.

This use of props and visual elements to provide a structure within the structure can enhance a Story Play at quite a deep level. If a Setting or Character Play relies on plot these same comments apply. Because the audience will be paying close attention to the clear, through-line structure of the plot, the visual elements will often work quite discreetly on them, but in an emotionally involving way that enriches the play. With a Setting Play — and a Character Play done in episodic style — the visual aspects have to be integral to the structure and development of the work. A few well-chosen props, costumes or slides can form the backbone of the play's structure and enable scenes to jump from one period to another or from one story to another without weakening the play's skeleton.

It is so important to engage the eyes of the audience as well as their minds and hearts. This is why, maybe paradoxically, I tend to discourage the use of fixed sets, especially with Theme Plays and the episodic style of play. When a play relies on a structure of many short scenes and a thread of theme, you might think that a fixed set would provide continuity and backbone. However, a fixed set does not provide you with the flexibility of weaving many visual elements into one large pattern. Weaving sub-structures of visual elements through the main structure of a play is more dynamic and satisfying.

It is also much harder to achieve and represents yet another ball to be juggled. But it's so exciting when the juggling works.

In *Childmyth* we used a structure that began with myths and historical material about children and childhood. The structure then expanded into the ideas and feelings of the cast about their status as kids and opened out even further into an attempt to create myths for now and the future: a megaphone-shaped play, in fact. A lot of this later work relied on movement and much of the structure and cohesion of the play relied on repeated visual patterns. One was of floating cloths. A large sheet of material held by two or more kids would float up into the air and then descend like a parachute, billowing as the corners were anchored. We used this in the historical scenes to create a god by placing a boy under the billowing yellow cloth which fell about him to create a richly patterned cloak. Later a billowing cloth was used as a net to catch a small boy who had been thrown through the air. In the final scenes the billowing cloths were used in conjunction with chants to establish a feeling of springtime ritual and re-birth. This repeated image linked all the periods of the play thematically and emotionally.

The visual patterning of a play also applies to movement on stage. Formal movement and dance scenes are choreographed but a lot of other movement on stage can be woven into substructures of the play. Entrances and exits can become repeated motifs. A character may reveal much by always entering in the same way and with the same people. Traffic patterns can establish the status of groups or individuals and movement can become a 'signature tune' for a character.

In *Piece by Piece*, scenes of argument were interspersed with scenes of formal presentation of ideas. The violent and natural movement into the arguments made them seem quite real. Many audience members thought the first argument which arose out of the set-up of the play was in fact real and that the cast had made a blunder. This was a very emotional moment that fixed a movement image in the audience's minds. That pattern of movement was then used to establish every argument and the audience reacted thereafter every time the cast began to move into an argument; a reaction of frustration that so many situations do lead to argument. The formal movement of other scenes established a pattern of presenting considered statements about peace; the more formal the movement, the more frightening the scenes tended to be. These two movement patterns set up a sub-structure of tension and intensity within the overall structure of the play.

FIRST AND LAST SCENES

In the structuring process you must test thoroughly the scenes that begin and end the play. Sometimes their creation will not have occurred during the workshop process — a common feature of building episodic plays — and you may need to develop these scenes at the structuring stage of the work. They need to be the most appropriate scenes in the play. A play can survive a structural question or even weakness in the middle, but if the first scene doesn't really begin the play and the last scene doesn't really end the play, you will have a very dissatisfied audience.

The first scene has to open the play to all sorts of dramatic possibilities while at the same time defining the theme and style. An audience will want to have a fairly good idea of the path they are to take so they are in tune with the action. But they also enjoy feeling that they are in for a few surprises and the style and energy of the first scene should excite their expectations.

The first scene is also very important for the cast. The stronger their first appearance is, the better they grab the audience, the more clearly the first scene establishes the play's themes, the easier the job is for the cast in the long haul of the performance. If that first scene works and the cast can feel that the audience is with them, the rest of the performance will take on energy and power. Coming back from an unclear and lacklustre first scene is a difficult job for any performer.

I sometimes suggest beginning a play with a mad burst of confused energy and ideas which leads into clarification at the end of the scene. This can suggest to an audience that the play will do the same thing. This is not a bad overall structure for an episodic play and it is a strong structure for a first scene. In *How to use a Machete in a Concrete Jungle*, the first scene set up the furniture for the play while the cast argued about where everything had to go. There was lots of noise and shoving of desks, etc. The Teacher, played by the group's real teacher, came on, yelled at them and showed them where everything should go with a few barked commands. They put the stuff in place rapidly and sat in position for the next scene.

This first scene established our set, let the audience look at our performers, set up a feeling of chaos resolved and introduced our surprise cast member, the real teacher. It also established our theme about people being pushed around by authority figures. The audience was immediately captured, amused and intrigued.

Giving the cast real jobs to do to bring them on stage can help the confidence of the group. Setting up the props and set of a play as a first scene can also be an interesting event for the audience, especially if they see the more novel props being laid out. There has to be something else happening as well, of course, unless the props and set are amazingly exciting. In *Piece by Piece*, the setting up involved business with a chair which fixed its position in the audience's mind as being very significant. When this led to an argument just as the cast were about to sing their first song, the audience had their suspicions confirmed. What appeared at first as inefficiency on the part of the cast turned into the first major thematic point of the play when the chair was taken off the stage to resolve the argument: 'No chair, no argument.' The chair was not used in the play again.

Try to ensure that any words or action that start a play are fairly simple to perform. In *Love Matters*, Melanie had only to say, 'Nobody loves me'. When a more substantial job of performance is needed you must be sure that the person doing it is very confident and competent. You can sometimes structure help into the scene. In *Baby Teeth*, the Dental Hygienist had to make a major speech to introduce the play. She had this speech on her clipboard and read it out, as if at a conference. In the background, the other twenty-odd cast members were positioning themselves and one boy was having his stomach painted.

A group song is a high energy, poetic and audience-pleasing way to begin a play. This will also introduce all your cast and can offer individual performance moments. The broad, emotional appeal of a song opens the play out effectively and the words can be used to plant ideas and themes firmly in the audience's minds.

The opening scene must open up the play but the closing scene should not close off the play. The last scene should provide a feeling of dramatic satisfaction for the audience, a feeling that the show has been rounded off well. But it is also important to leave intriguing possibilities or a lingering image or idea, so that the play works on the audience even after it has finished. That effect will mostly be achieved by the impact of the overall play and by the quality of the ideas and performances, but the last scene is the final opportunity to drive home the play's themes and ideas.

An ending that returns to the beginning of the play can be very effective in giving a rounded-off feeling while leaving openness for reflection, because it brings the audience back to the root of the play's argument. The return to the beginning should have some variation so that new thinking is prodded. With *S.K.Y.*, the second-last scene suggested that the problem had been solved so that the last scene, repeating the first but with two new kids hit by falling sky, re-opened all the discussion and asked new questions about adult assurances, while dramatically completing the play.

The powerful, lingering image creates an ending that I particularly like. If you can find the right image, the play can ring in memories for a long time. *Dancing With Kangaroos* offered a powerful image with the cast spread across the stage with bright umbrellas held high. *The Playground Re-Play* focused on the dead Rebel, cradled in the arms of the Outsider. These final images are often echoes or developed versions of other strong visual elements in the play, and it is possible to build these 'snapshot' images towards a final image. When this is done well the lingering effect of the play through its series of images becomes almost haunting.

A final song can be an excellent way to end the play. The song can be created to carry a poetic summary of the main themes and the music of a final song provides a satisfying, emotional rounding-off for a play. It may be that you will choose to reprise a song that is very significant within the play and you will then gain the benefits of echoes as well as a nice finish.

It is not often dramatic, however, to offer a summing up at the end, unless it is in a song in which the music has a poetic and emotional effect. Most summary scenes tend to lack dramatic energy and certainly lack emotion. It is nearly impossible to say that something cannot work in theatre, but it is a common error of casts to think audiences may need to be reminded of the important points. I would suggest that you never pander to this fear. If the fear should prove to be correct then it is the whole play that needs attention, not just the last scene.

Technical Elements and Blackouts

Any element used in a show can become an important part of the structural pattern. If a TV segment is used only once, it still has to be placed to complement the overall structure of the play. Technical aspects of a show must be placed carefully to avoid any damage to the human control over the structure. As with complex set-ups or entrances, there may need to be something else happening on stage to cover smooth flow into a technical moment. With careful rehearsal there is no reason why technical aspects of a play cannot enhance the structure and even offer a sub-structure of their own with appropriate rhythm and placement. The fact that it rarely happens that way in my experience should not be a total discouragement but a strong warning.

Again, I would advise against using blackouts to control the structure of a play. The structure should be clearly and firmly in the hands of the cast, otherwise you water down their most significant experience in playbuilding: learning to control and manipulate creative structure.

Most of playbuilding is straight-forward hard work, all made worthwhile by the chance to practise those few hours of artistry when you make the play into a structure that is greater than the sum of its parts. Do not be afraid to experiment and try out different scene orders in rehearsal. This will often reveal connections and strengths you may not have thought about. It is worth the effort of trial and error to be sure that the play has the best framework. As soon as the structure of a play begins to work, the pleasure and sense of achievement for all the group will lift all the work to a much higher level. Those few workshops in which you all struggle to make a collection of scenes into a real play are nervewracking and draining, but the final sense of achievement is worth it all.

Young people are not often given the chance to deal with the structuring of events or major creative works, so have little experience in how to do it. This is why it is so important that they have the chance to be involved in all the structuring work in playbuilding. And also why the director will usually have the strongest voice in that work. Ensure that your voice is not autocratic and that you do explain and discuss all the steps and reasons behind the structuring decisions. These explanations and discussions provide, arguably, the most vital and lasting lessons young people will learn from you in the playbuilding process.

SUMMARY

- Allow the material to shape the play.
- The structure must propel the drama.
- Discuss and analyse the play's structure with the group. Experiment with the structure.
- Practical needs — Casting, stage-traffic, costumes, props — will shape much of the play.
- Make a scene list including cast for each scene and time of each scene. Juggle all the elements into a practical pattern. Try several patterns.
- Avoid awkward links between scenes. Cover set-ups with an out-front scene.
- The better the cast understand the emotional, intellectual and dramatic patterns of the play, the better they do their jobs.

- Balance in a play means a sense of harmony and aptness, not necessarily symmetry. Balancing all the elements of a play is like creating a fine poem, a symphony or weaving a beautiful carpet.
- Balancing can mean separating similar elements, such as songs and poems for variety, or placing similar scenes close together to achieve echo effects.
- Visualising an overall shape for the play — megaphone; hour-glass; circle; straight-line — may help you place scenes.
- Time taken for each scene can be used to structure pace and rhythm into a play.
- Shifting *contrast* of mood, time, ideas, cast size, style, etc will keep an audience interested, alert and surprised. But don't make the play too busy.
- *Repeated patterns and echoes* in ideas, movement, visuals, groupings, etc, form a hidden sub-structure to the play.
- Weaving sub-structures of visual elements through the main structure can be more dynamic and satisfying for an audience than a fixed set and cast movement can also hold repeated patterns and echoes beyond any definite choreography.
- *First and last scenes* must be thoroughly tested in the structuring period. They may need to be specifically created at this time.
- The first scene must open the play to dramatic possibilities while defining thematic and stylistic areas of the play. Its success is vital for the confidence of the cast.
- Some first scene suggestions: chaos resolved; setting up the show; real jobs to do; a group song.
- The last scene should not close off the play but round it off, leaving lingering images and ideas.
- Some last scene suggestions: a return to the first scene with variations; lingering image/tableau; a song. Avoid summing up.
- Technical aspects must be carefully placed to avoid any damage to the human control over the structure.
- Experiment with the structure. Test and analyse the final structure rigorously. Keep testing it with audience reaction.

LOVE MATTERS

This project was interesting in the way it developed through a number of difficulties. It illustrates well the guidelines I have noted in all chapters so far. The project was under great pressure from the beginning because a group of twelve young people — aged from twelve to twenty-one — had been selected at Shopfront to create two plays to tour overseas at the end of 1988, Australia's Bicentennial year. The plays were to be performed in Prague, Paris, York, London and some regional centres in Britain. This made it quite hard to get ideas from the group at first because they kept censoring themselves with the thought, 'Is this idea important enough for an overseas tour?'

This lack of confidence can occur with any first-time project but is especially likely when a major event — going to a festival; touring to other schools; appearing on TV; etc — is planned before the play is created. This group were mostly inexperienced in playbuilding but had done considerable work on scripted shows. Although they were all talented performers, their confidence in their ability to create two plays worthy of the tour was quite low. They were also under a lot of pressure between rehearsals in running fund-raising projects for the tour.

Some practical parameters helped our process. We had decided that the major play must be about their view of Australia in some way. People would expect this in Bicentennial year and we felt it was a good theme to show overseas. So this second play could be a bit shorter and maybe a bit more fun, I told them. We had decided that it should be a Theme Play, typical of Shopfront's playbuilding work. But it was not until the third session that the group decided upon the theme of love for their play.

We had seven months to do the work, which sounds like a long time. But this was actually thirty sessions — all day on Sundays — to create two major shows and polish them to a very high standard. Although some work could be done by individuals during the week — finding poems and other material; writing music; etc — the ensemble nature of the work restricted most of it to Sundays. Because all of us were very aware that the work had to be 'worthy', progress was very slow. But this wariness induced a method of work in which the group demanded of me that each step and scene be meticulously developed with great attention to performance detail as we went. This tended to inhibit the free-flowing nature of the playbuilding but was vital to their confidence as a group. It brought the direction element of playbuilding into force much earlier than usual.

Our first two improvisations were ideas tossed up simply to prove that they could actually improvise effectively. This group's lack of confidence in their ability to improvise is a good example of why it is so important to do playbuilding with young people before taking them into scripted work. The playbuilding gives them confidence in their creativity for all drama work. I suggested to the group that we pick two locations for two 'love situations'.

The style of the scenes they created was from TV and the situations rather cliched, but it was a start and demonstrated that they could create an interesting piece of drama from virtually nothing. Seeking personal experiences and views for the play — despite the fact that the group had agreed that they would like the play to be more personal than general — was still quite hard, as the thought of exposing themselves to the whole wide world remained daunting.

However, from this point of first scene creation the hard work of gradually drawing out ideas and of testing the quality of the ideas steadily progressed. The group's confidence grew as their play grew. We finally had a play that was confronting, funny and entertaining. While we saw it as our 'fun' piece for the tour, teachers and students in Britain commented on the honesty of the play, on the relevance it had to other young people and on its uncompromising treatment of issues. These qualities came from the strength of the playbuilding process which had assessed and analysed the work constantly.

After the play's Sydney season, changes were discussed and a scene omitted. Before our first performance in Czechoslovakia we omitted another scene — an extended joke that never quite seemed to work — shortened the song that was based on Shakespeare's Sonnet 130, and changed the beginning of the play slightly.

Scenario for LOVE MATTERS

Touring production by Shopfront Theatre. Cast and creators: Lynne Atkinson; Andrew Brook; Jamie Campbell; Michael Daly; Melanie Hughes; Nick Jordan; David Malek; Alice Moore; Signa Reddy; David Rendell; Nichole Sullivan; Luke Tebbutt; with E. B. as director.

The set was nine chairs, sturdy enough to stand on.

NOBODY LOVES ME   Melanie, who is twelve, walks out and tells the audience, 'Nobody loves me'. The others enter and tell her, 'I'm your sister; I love you.' 'I'm your teacher; it's my job to love you.' 'Shut up, Melanie; I'm your brother and I love you.' The third person on stage is David R, the oldest in the group, and he tells the audience, 'Love doesn't exist anyway'. Finally, everyone is frustrated by Melanie and shouts at her, 'We all love you!' Pointing at Nick, who has been sitting reading a Playboy magazine, she says, 'He doesn't love me'.

(Note: 'No-one loves me' and 'Love doesn't exist' became continuing motifs. The *Playboy* was used in many scenes, sometimes as a menu or a ladder catalogue. In Sydney, we had a problem at first with the opening scene: Melanie never got a laugh on what we thought was a good punchline. The reason was that we had opened the scene with Melanie and David coming on together and David had made a few comments about love not existing. This had set a tone of seriousness which inhibited the audiences from laughing. When we re-structured the scene to the above, we got our laugh every time.)

BEAUTY   Luke announces he is an artist and wants to draw true beauty. He selects Melanie. She poses and he draws as the scene continues. A Legs Contest for boys is announced. The girls are to be judges. Each boy drops his trousers — long shirts underneath — and his legs are inspected. When David R goes to drop his pants the girls say, 'Don't bother.' Andrew is judged the best and gets a First Prize sash to wear. As he does up his pants, he confides to the audience, 'I hate being a sex symbol.' Luke shows his drawing. It is of Melanie's foot.

The Eyes Contest is announced and they all line up. Ziggy inspects the eyes and then plucks them out and drops them in a dish Jamie carries. The blinded person puts on sunglasses. Jamie begins to eat the eyes. Mike tries to flatter Ziggy but still loses his eyes. Ziggy and Jamie then shout out parts of the body and the group show these off in a quick movement pattern. 'Feet! Legs! Eyes! Bottoms! Shoulders! Hair!' This builds into a chant and the group marches to and fro on the stage in unison until they are shouting. They then drop to their knees and quietly sing Sonnet 130, which begins, 'My mistress' eyes are nothing like the sun'.

(Note: We chose to place a highly symbolic and stylised scene early in the play to let the audience know that we were concerned with general issues about love and to jolt their preconceptions about what a play on love should be. The legs section was important in this. The eye-gouging — and-eating, which always got a shocked laugh, also shook up the audience's thinking processes. The shouts of the body parts contrasted well with the softness of the song.)

SONNET 130   By Shakespeare. Sung to flute. At the end the cast take off their glasses as they begin to move off-stage.

THE FOLDER   Andrew gets his folder and spreads out pictures, magazine articles and papers — all about love. He reads, 'All love is sweet, Given or returned. Common as light is love, And its familiar voice wearies not ever.' David M asks what the folder is for. Andrew is trying to understand love. David M says that lots of girls at school like Andrew. But Andrew insists he wants to know all about love before he gets involved in it. David M says, 'I've got a girlfriend and we love each other. You're stuck here on your own with a folder'.

PROPOSAL   Alice walks on saying, 'I love you', followed by Nichole. Alice says, 'I love you' in lots of different ways. The others come on and offer advice. Meanwhile Andrew packs up his folder and leaves. She goes to Luke and tells him she loves him, as the others watch. He is embarrassed and says he'll see her later and walks away. She cries and the others beat Luke up for hurting her feelings. Luke is left spread-eagled face-down on the floor. He looks up weakly and tells the audience, 'I love her too.'

ASHLEY   Andrew announces, 'Ashley, aged two'. Four of the cast go to Luke and lift him high in the air, each holding a limb, bringing him down on his feet, standing upright as others attach long rods to his hands and feet. They then manipulate him like a stick puppet in some parts of the scene. The scene — in many brief segments — shows Ashley growing up and how love is used to manipulate his life and attitudes. His parents give him toys when he says he loves them. On his first day at school, his mother asks, 'Aren't you going to cry?' His little friends play at mummies and daddies. One wants to be the lady next door who loves the daddy because 'that's what happened to my dad'. The loud uncle teases Ashley about Melanie being his girlfriend. Melanie announces that she has a girlfriend and that they love each other and kiss each other. Mum and Dad cover Ashley's eyes and ears and get her out of the house. At thirteen, Mum and Dad pick a nice, quiet girl for him, rejecting older girls whom Ashley likes. Jamie, who played the Dad, then becomes Ashley at sixteen. The puppeteers move him into position in his bedroom with the *Playboy* magazine. His Mum sees him and tells Dad (now Mike) that he had better give Ashley a little talk. Dad tries to be very cheery as he tells Ashley he'd better practise a bit before he gets married but not too soon and he must use lots of protection. Now Ashley is even more puzzled. His friend has a girl lined up for him at a party but when the girl asks him to go upstairs, Ashley says no and goes home to his room and his *Playboy*. Ashley is now 19 and at university where he meets an older woman, a tutor, who tells him how much she likes younger men. As he leans towards her, seven of the cast rush and hold him back. But Ashley breaks through and as he goes off, the Narrator asks, 'Free? At last? Or is he?' And the others follow Ashley in close formation. Mum and Dad are left. Mum says, 'We never see Ashley much any more'. Dad says, 'No. Children forget their parents and all the love we give them'.

EVERYBODY'S LOVE   The music begins off-stage as Mum and Dad exit. The chorus goes, 'This is
SONG   my song to make you love me, This is my song to make you cry. But you never do.' Combined with rather silly but fun dancing and tableaux, they sing about different types of love. Words were by E.B. with music by Andrew Brook.

(Note: Originally the song gave everyone a verse but it was much too long and the quality of the song was not good enough to sustain such length. We cut it by almost two-thirds after a couple of performances.)

THE LADDER SHOP   As the cast walk away at the end of the song, Ziggy says to Mike, 'Excuse me, I need a ladder'. Lynne then bursts into a sexy rendition of 'The Ladder Shop Song' (words David Rendell; music Lynne Atkinson) setting the soapie style of the scene. The chorus and Lynne sing their way off stage. The story was complex and was presented at rapid-fire pace with exaggerated soapie acting. Mike and Alice work in the shop. Alice bursts into tears constantly. Mike uses the Playboy as a ladder catalogue. Alice shows Melanie how to test a ladder. David M wants Mike to serve him. Alice cries. Luke enters and attracts David M's attention. Melanie falls from her ladder. Mike leaps on her to give mouth-to-mouth resuscitation. Jamie enters and sees his girlfriend being kissed by Mike. Ziggy slaps Jamie who is her husband. He falls down and Alice gives him mouth-to-mouth. Nick enters and sees Ziggy who is his long-lost mother. She faints. Neither Luke nor David M will give her mouth-to-mouth and Nick can't to his own mother. David R enters with heavy accent as the Mysterious Stranger. He leaps on Ziggy and gives her mouth-to-mouth. Nick faints. Luke and David M fight over who will give him mouth-to-mouth — both want to. Andrew enters with Nichole and Luke recognises him as a star from 'Neighbours' and faints. Nichole leaps on Nick and David M leaps on Luke. All are now on the floor in 'kissing' positions, except Andrew who asks, 'Doesn't anyone want my autograph?' Enter Miss Bitch who demands service. Everyone leaps up. Miss Bitch comments on Andrew's coke habit and that his wife is still molesting children. She demands a ladder, 'and make it a big one', she tells Mike. The Mysterious Stranger oils his way off. Nick and Ziggy leave together, happy. Miss Bitch and Nichole have a slanging match. Jamie wipes away her tears. Miss Bitch says he is an embezzler. Melanie screams. Melanie tells him he'll never see her body again if he isn't in the car in ten seconds. Jamie rushes his goodbyes to Nichole as he counts off the seconds. Andrew has been signing autographs for the boys. He and Nichole leave. David M goes to Mike about buying a ladder. Miss Bitch goes to Luke. She tells him she wants him but he says he must first tell her his terrible secret. He does a little dance around the room as he keeps saying, joyfully, 'I'm gay; I'm gay; I'm gay. ' David M goes to him and asks if he wants to go for a coffee. They do. Alice laughs at Miss Bitch who storms out. The song starts up in the background as off-stage Announcer asks what will happen next time in The Ladder Shop. Mike and Alice meanwhile have thrown themselves into each other's arms: 'Alone, at last. '

(Note: This scene is a good example of persistent playbuilding. It began as something of an exercise and several times in the process the group considered dropping it altogether because it was so hard to create. It became a challenge which carried over into our other playbuilding. Finally, through dogged editing and analysis, we included all the cast in the scene and honed all the jokes. The scene became the high point of the play.)

RUNNING AWAY Neighbouring families have daughters who have trouble with their brothers — both brothers are named David. Melanie is pushed into the background because of David. Nichole is in constant disagreement with her David. Both decide to run away. Melanie leaves a note. They meet in the street and Nichole, being older, persuades Melanie to go back. Melanie agrees so long as they both return. When they do, they are met with loud abuse from all members of each family. The end of the scene is patterned so that both sets of parents speak in unison, ending on, 'Go to your room. '

MELANIE'S SONG

Freeze. Melanie steps out of the freeze to speak her song direct to the audience.
(Words by E. B. from workshop discussion; music by Andrew Brook.) Melanie tells how lonely it feels when you're not loved. Even kids need to be loved. Halfway through the song the others move and quietly set up for the next scene. 'Sometimes I think I might die and never have been loved.' She walks off slowly.

COFFEE SHOP

Luke and David M come on as their characters from the Ladder Shop scene. They order and argue. Mike enters and orders. Nick is the Waiter. The *Playboy* is the menu. David R, Lynne, Andrew and Nichole enter. The actions and conversations keep changing focus, pairing people up in different combinations. Mike joins them — making a play for anyone who'll have him and Lynne makes eyes at the Waiter. Finally, Mike asks them all to go back to his place to watch a video. They all stand, then Mike pairs with Lynne, Andrew with Nichole, and David R with the Waiter. Every couple then has a gentle punchline to get them off stage. 'Leo! I bet you're a Leo. Gemini? Aries?' Lynne and Mike are left and she begins her song.

LYNNE'S SONG

The song asks how come a great person like her has got stuck with a no-hoper like Mike? The only answer is, 'I love him'. The song is humorous but Mike gets cranky about it. Finally he demands, 'You finished singing so we can go?' and storms off. She follows, lovingly.

(Note: This song was added late in the process when the group realised that Lynne had no song to sing. As she was a very good singer, the group suggested I write a song for her. We discussed the theme of the song and we knew it should come at this point as there was something of a hole here. Andrew wrote and played the music. Even later, the Ladder Shop Song was created for Lynne to improve the style and shape of the Ladder Shop scene.)

BREAK UP

Alice and David M enter, arguing. He loves her but she doesn't want to be his steady girl. Andrew begins laying out his folder papers again. Alice wants to see other boys but David M says it's all or nothing. Alice says, 'That suits me fine' and walks away. David M turns to Andrew.

FOLDER 2

David M asks if the folder can advise him what to do now he's lost someone he loves. Andrew says that the folder really tells you nothing. He's fed up with it. He asks David M who are the girls who like him. He then goes off 'to make some phone calls'. David M sits with the folder. He reads the quote again, 'All love is sweet, Given or returned. Common as light is love, And its familiar voice wearies not ever'. A quiet pause.

BLUES 130

Nick bounces on and announces, 'Our finale'. Nichole and the Nickettes sing 'Blues 130'. This is a raucous blues version of Sonnet 130 with all the cast involved, except David M who looks through his folder. The song ends with whoops and hollers as they all go off. David M has packed up the folder and, as he leaves with it, he repeats the last words of the song — 'False compare'.

END

Only Melanie (the youngest) and David R (the oldest) are left. He holds out his arm to her and asks, 'Shall we go, love?' She says, 'Why not, love?' They walk off arm-in-arm as lights fade. There is no bow.

(Note: There is a triple echo at the end — the quiet poem, the song, which has the same words but is energetic and rather wild, and the words, 'False compare'. There is a reverse echo with David M now holding the love folder. And the play finishes with Melanie — the 'no-one loves me' girl who began the play — making something of a positive change with the ambiguous, 'Why not love?' The last three scenes are larger echoes because all have been done before, in a slightly different form, near the beginning of the play. It is of interest to note that this play was performed to fifteen different school audiences around Britain and all related quite strongly to the issues of the play.)

CHAPTER 7

DIRECTING AND PRESENTING THE PLAY

Every director will have a personal style and approach to directing. But in playbuilding you are dealing with a very specific directing task, especially when the work is with young people, and you must tailor your skills to that job. You are not taking a script and applying your interpretation or trying to project clearly one playwright's view. Your directing must take into account, more than usual, a number of attitudes and ideas. You must link your directing abilities to the needs of the kids and their play.

Direction begins from the first session and becomes a greater component of the work as the creation progresses. In the final few sessions the work will probably be almost all rehearsal, with the director being almost totally a Theatre Director, and very little creation of new material will occur. The approach to directing the performance aspects of the play should come from the methods and attitudes used by the director in guiding the creation of the play. There must not be a sudden change from leader, encourager, enthuser into autocratic Director. Sometimes I tell my groups that I now have to be more pushy because we are shaping a performance and that needs firm direction. But, because the material belongs to the group, there is greater need for collaboration in the direction process than may normally occur in theatre.

As director, accept that you probably know more about theatre than anyone else in the group, so it is quite reasonable for you to assert a certain level of expertise. The group must accept that in some difficult decisions your opinion is more likely to be right than theirs. If the playbuilding process has been positive and productive the group will trust your abilities as a director and that will make decision-making easier for you. The directing aspects of the process will happen more quickly than the creative aspects and you need the group's confidence to follow you at some speed when it comes to polishing, balancing and shaping all the work into an effective performance. Their confidence in you will enable you to direct within a personal style and inject some of your own artistic beliefs and feelings about their play into the work. But as you work at speed you must not forget to take note of all opinions and feelings expressed by the group about the direction of the play. If you do not you will speedily lose their confidence and trust. It is easy to become a monster when you start to direct and have all those final pressures of time and standards to deal with. But nobody benefits from having a monster direct them.

Be generous in your directing. Give the play to the performers. Make it theirs by directing them more firmly into their strengths and by providing support in their areas of weakness. Do not swamp the play with gimmicks. Challenge your cast to hold all the reins and to keep the play disciplined and controlled through their own work, their own skills and their own personalities. If the group has not come out of the creating process with enough discipline, you may like to style the play so that all the cast remains on stage throughout the show. This will increase the need for discipline and for them to keep a clear focus in the play at all times. The style will make the need fully apparent to the group and they will respond to that.

When a group has created something they want to say, even need to say, they will eagerly seek direction so that they can present their work well. This is when direction is the most effective, when the group perceives the need for it. So let them know what you are doing; how you plan to style the show; what input they should make; how their responses to your work can now make the show wonderful instead of ordinary. If you do not have a solution to a problem, ask for help. If you make a mistake, admit it and correct it. You and the group are full partners in this enterprise but the biggest responsibility is now falling on you to make the show the best it can be.

Your job now as director is to help the cast lift their performances and to ensure that the play is focused at all times, has pace and rhythm, has enough contrast, has an effective structure, makes sense, and above all is entertaining. All this is achieved by constant explanation to the cast of how the play is working as a piece of theatre, so that they fully understand what is needed. If they only understand how to do things 'by numbers' then they have no control over the play.

KIDS AND AMATEURS

Yes, it is true that your cast are kids and amateurs. We must face up to this and not pretend to ourselves that the kids are 'as good as professionals'. (If you are, in fact, playbuilding with professional actors, still read on. I think these comments will be useful for you as well.) But do not think of this status as imposing limitations; it should be seen in the light of boundary lines, indicating the area within which the performance must operate. Professional actors have limits and force boundary lines on a director too. And 'kid' and 'amateur' should be seen as positive terms. They depict a type of energy, exuberance and commitment that is rare in professional actors. Use those qualities. Give the cast clearly appointed work to do on stage. They may not be able to bring the skills and training of a professional actor to a performance but they can bring professional work practices. You must encourage and urge that at all times.

Encouraging your performers to think always in terms of the work is the best way to free them and protect them against disaster. Doing jobs on stage frees the cast by providing security and confidence. By the time the performance occurs they will have the security of knowing they can efficiently achieve all the work that is needed to make the play a success. If something goes wrong — and it almost always does — they will have the ability to correct and control the mistakes because they know so well what is needed for the play.

The cast should be able to do their jobs so easily that there is no need for nerves or any unpleasant sense of panic on stage. Being able to do the jobs well seems to expand time, so that time to deal with problems is easily fitted into the work. It also allows the performers to expand their abilities for performance and you often see some real acting come out of the kids. But the kids must understand that the 'artistry' they yearn for can only come when the 'craft' aspects are efficiently in place.

Playbuilding deals very well with kids and amateurs because it is the theatrical form that makes a complex art readily available to the ordinary person. Anyone can speak through the theatre arts by using play-building — and speak well and entertainingly. My colleague Garry Fry created a play with blind people about their everyday lives. It was funny and moving, and it told their story, which they had never been able to tell in an effective form before. Playbuilding gave them a voice. Faye Westwood created a beautiful Story Play with mentally handicapped kids who showed it at Shopfront to over one hundred of their peers from other Special Schools. The play was an inspiration to the kids, their teachers and their parents. Faye went on to do several successful playbuilding projects with handicapped children. Too often theatre is regarded as a specialist art form that only the 'professionals' can present properly. This relegates everyone else to being passive. Playbuilding empowers anyone to do theatre well — not like a professional, but like a committed, efficient amateur who has something to say.

Kids-and-amateurs bring lots of qualities to theatre, especially a freshness of view and a sense of humour that stamps their work as being original, raw and from the heart. Many times you will also see — especially in young people — a lot of natural acting and performance talent. Kids with talent are attracted to performance projects so that should not be surprising. But it can present directing problems because you will want to give the talented ones the best opportunity to show their talents. Do not let your pleasure in their revealed talents and your commitment to their project distort your judgement of their weaknesses and strengths. Encourage them to go beyond the point that they think they can reach, but be realistic.

PROTECTION

Protection is one of the most important jobs you have as director. Protection does not involve packing the group in cotton wool and most certainly does not mean protecting them from honourable failure. But you should protect them from deserved failure in public. If the show deserves to fail, it should not be allowed to go on. If the group has not worked hard enough to reach an acceptable standard then they must be told so and no audience should have the play inflicted on them. This rarely happens and, if it does, you should take a hard look at your playbuilding process.

An honourable failure is a learning experience that has to be analysed, discussed and built upon. Almost every play you do will have moments of honourable failure, moments of exhilarating success and lots of moments of ordinary theatrical pleasure. Sometimes there are boring bits and always people will nominate different favourite scenes. You do not often get something as good as *King Lear* when you playbuild but you rarely get a total disaster. Because the playbuilt show is usually for a specific purpose or occasion, it reaches for immediacy rather than greatness. And it is theatre for everyone, not for an elite. Many parents will remember the lessons and insights they received long after they have forgotten what the play was about. The kids will grow from the experience long after they have forgotten the show.

Be honest and be consistent. These are the best protections for your group. Being honest does not mean being brutal, of course. The callous and casual comment about people's abilities or ideas is never helpful. Being honest can mean helping a kid to present a song well even though you have said, 'You don't sing strongly enough to hold the stage with this.' The next step after that comment is, 'Do you really want to do it or will we give it to someone else?' The next step, if the kid wants to do it, is to help make the performance acceptable. If that is impossible, you have to help them decide to drop the idea or the scene.

False encouragement can be as damaging as callous criticism. It is only when faults or weaknesses are admitted that effective work can be undertaken to correct or improve them. I make a point of praising my groups individually and collectively as often as possible. By praising their strengths you will find that the weaknesses improve as well. My groups always know that I will tell them when their work is good and that I will always mean it. This is a considerable security and protection for the group. I give them a high standard to strive for and they know they will be told when they are near it, when they hit it and when they surpass the standard.

Baby Teeth.

Without being dishonest, it is important to keep up the spirits of the kids as you approach performance. If you are unhappy about the way the show is at the last rehearsal, but do not intend to cancel it and you have no more time for rehearsal, then you must keep your frustrations to yourself. Find all the positive things to say and urge them to lift the work in performance. This is what happens with theatre productions everywhere. The point of difference with playbuilding is that you are dealing with a group who are not only performers but also creators of the work. Double sensitivity is required.

The final protection in your role of director is to leave the performance to them. Your job is to sit up the back — never sit down the front where they can see you and keep checking your reactions to their work — and to watch the show and the audience. I never give notes after the first night of a run because that is a time when they should relax and enjoy the fact that the whole thing happened. But I do give notes before the second performance and then after each show. The notes are only on significant points and not too many. Notes should include praise, of course. Giving notes also shows the group that you are doing your job as they must do theirs and that you are still committed to the show even though it is now fully in their hands.

PRACTICAL DIRECTING

Some of these matters are issues of personal style but remember that a young group may need a special approach. Again, I emphasise how much can be achieved by concentrating the efforts on the jobs that need to be done on stage and backstage. It is not much use talking about pace and rhythm in performance until all the jobs can be done smoothly and well. In fact, by emphasising efficiency you can begin to develop a sense of rhythm in their work and a consciousness of the pleasure of rhythm. If several people need to set up a scene, encourage them to do it with patterns of movement and a rhythm that makes a plain job become an aesthetic moment, even though a background to the main action.

In *Piece by Piece*, the first scene was the set-up of props. The job had to be done efficiently because all the props had to be in their right places so the play could happen. This meant that the cast were immediately doing something real and something that the audience could perceive as a job. But the audience also knew it was the start of a play. The positioning of a chair was to lead to an argument just as the play proper began, so instead of having someone simply place the chair, I asked several of them to move the chair from place to place, each making a point of carefully positioning it. This required no acting but did need timing and a sense of the pace and rhythm of the scene.

Placing yourself is a practical task too. In early sessions when discussion is paramount, I sit in close with the group. When scenes are being created and the middle period of work occurs, I move in and out from observation point to discussion point. If the director is too close during an improvisation, it can inhibit the work. When we reach the directing period and the scenes are being put together I sit as far away from them as possible, most of the time. This enables me to see patterns being created in the space and encourages them to speak up and project voices. It also suggests the gradual removal of the director from the project.

It is practical to give the performers time and space to develop their own skills and intuitions about a scene before becoming too specific in your directions. Try to avoid showing them how to perform any part of the play. Showing can lead to mindless copying. But it is sometimes necessary for a director to demonstrate physically positions or actions. Just take care to do this as seldom as possible and to discourage copying of your own performance style.

I think it is perfectly practical to ask for more than the group thinks they can achieve. It seems impractical not to. Without a standard, the group can flounder about aimlessly when it comes to rehearsals. Set a high but reasonable standard and then direct your group towards it. When you are certain they will reach that standard, it does not hurt to raise it further — praising them at the same time. Setting challenging standards should occur in all aspects of the work. It is the most practical way of achieving excellent results.

PRESENTATIONAL (OR BRECHTIAN) ACTING

Broadly there are three basic acting styles: declamatory, where you orate and gesture in grand style; naturalistic or realistic, where you try to be as much like real-life as possible; presentational or Brechtian, where you demonstrate or present ideas and actions to an audience. There are, of course, many variations within these broad categories. Declamatory and naturalistic acting almost always require training or exceptional ability if they are to be convincing. Presentational acting is to my mind the most natural form of acting for the amateur because it is what all of us do whenever we tell a joke or a story or describe a person we met or a movie we saw. We use hands and voice to explain what the situation was like. Facial expressions and body movements are used to suggest the situation. We usually do not act out our stories fully for our 'audience' but we do present it packaged in a slightly more dramatic way than in normal conversation. Anyone can do it.

This is why in the very early workshops when people have ideas, I tell them, 'Show me'. The action of moving through a scene about something that happened at home last night is not far removed from that of telling an incident with a few hand gestures and occasional grimaces. Sometimes a kid will say, 'She was sitting around about where Kate is over there. So I went over.' And maybe I will interrupt and say, 'Well, just do it then and Kate can be the girl and just show us how it happened.'

Most 'acting' done by young people is naturally presentational, as described above. It would be possible to push their performance, say in the example above, into naturalistic acting but you are then pushing them into areas where they cannot easily excel. Presentational performance provides the best opportunity for very good performance work by kids and amateurs. The step into naturalistic acting is much greater and much harder. It involves all sorts of attention to fine detail and to psychological deliberations about inner selves. The psychology of presentational acting is mostly confined to actions and reactions and broad probabilities.

The portrayal of character and situation through presentational acting is just as convincing to an audience as with naturalistic acting. It is simply working in a different form. Audiences enjoy the flexibility that presentational acting gives to performers who can drop in and out of character easily, change character and add into a show a whole variety of theatrical elements not possible if a performer is locked into a naturalistic role. Presentational performance even allows the kids who can achieve a competent level of naturalistic acting to add this into the variety of their show.

Some directors aim to progress from presentational performance to naturalistic acting. I do not think this way because the step is not a natural one. The three styles of acting are discrete, not a hierarchy of excellence. The real development in drama with young people is to help them improve their abilities to perform in presentational style. Because this style is familiar to audiences it is more 'user friendly' in the theatre. It does not make audiences feel inexpert and separated from the performers. It is not a style to be viewed objectively or as 'art'; it is a style that promotes and welcomes real audience involvement and identification.

I urge all playbuilding directors to work in this area of the presentational. Add declamatory for fun and naturalistic for variety if you like but make the presentational your basic working style.

PACE AND RHYTHM

These two concepts are very hard for young people and inexperienced performers to grasp. Unfortunately — and I plead guilty on many occasions — playbuilt shows often do not achieve effective pace and rhythm. This is usually because rehearsal time becomes so limited — often time is stolen from the rehearsal period for more ideas work — and the group do not get enough run-throughs to give them a real feel for the shape and timing of their show. However, rewarding as it is to develop these qualities in our shows, it should be recognised that a playbuilt show can survive on good ideas, high energy and strong commitment. A developed sense of pace and rhythm is the icing on the cake; but the cake can still be edible without icing, so do not despair if your time runs out.

When a play is destined for a significant run of performances or for some specially important project, a big effort should be made to grasp pace and rhythm. These qualities will come in some scenes even as it is performed and will come from certain members of the group who have a feel for timing and flow. There are several ways to stimulate that instinct and to help the group understand what pace and rhythm can mean to a performance. The first way is to give these elements some attention as you develop the scenes. Sometimes it can be useful to select one particular scene where the rhythm can be used to advantage and then give that scene a lot of attention. That can act as an example that flows over into other scenes and the rest of the play will take less time.

When the final structuring of the play is near, I begin to emphasise the ideas of pace and rhythm. I spend some time discussing this with the group and use examples from TV, such as the pace of adventure shows or humorous shows, and from sport, such as the rhythm needed when running a distance race or the way you feel when you are playing a game really well, when all your movements are flowing into well-timed actions. It can also help to use the repeated patterns and echoes of the play as points from which to measure the pace and rhythm of the play.

There are three strategies I try when time permits. The first is to do a number of speed runs of the play. This means racing through the play in half the usual time while keeping it intelligible and making sure that everything is said and done as in a normal performance. This speeding up will reveal to them how various parts of the play respond to extra pace and how the absence of a reasonable rhythm is very noticeable. They should then be encouraged to reach for pacing and a sense of rhythm when they do a normal run-through, immediately after the speed run.

I use the walk and talk-through rehearsal as well. With this I ask the group to move into all their positions as in the play but to describe what they do and say in the play instead of really doing it and saying it. They move from spot to spot, telling their actions and words and becoming more aware of the presentational needs at each point. This also helps the group to grasp the themes of the play more fully. It also reminds them of the jobs they have to carry out on stage.

In some cases I actually use one or two run-throughs to 'conduct' the play. While the group do their rehearsals as normal, I walk up and down in front, or amongst them, talking at them constantly, telling them where a touch more pace would help; slow down there a bit; flow into the poem, flow, flow; lift the movements; the people at the back must be absolutely still so this front action will hold the focus; that arm movement was wonderful, can someone else echo that?; yes, stand on the chair; let the scene slide away now, slide it; a beat, a beat, we need the feel of a beat here. And so on. This conducting method can help with a number of problems but can only be done with the full understanding and co-operation of the group. The fact that they must keep the play going as if in performance while some half-crazed director walks up and down trying to conduct them like an orchestra, demanding that they listen to him while they are trying to listen to their play and work at it, is very good for concentration. The pressure of responding to two strong sets of stimuli and instructions at once can shake loose some of the bad and lazy habits that some people fall into and can help focus all minds on the idea of the play as a whole piece, as a symphony to be played to the audience. Conducting the play in an exercise like this will help stress the non-verbal, non-ideas aspects of the show and will sharpen awareness of pace and rhythm simply by giving so much unusual attention to them.

PROCESS AND PRODUCT

Once upon a time some drama teachers believed that it was bad to end up with a product from drama workshops with young people. That was some nasty thing called 'theatre' and arguments were put that showing the work somehow harmed both the kids and the benefits of the drama process. It has always seemed to me that if kids create something they are proud of — a painting, a poem, a play — they will want to show it to people and if you stop them you create an enormous confusion in their minds. Arguments about drama versus theatre, and process versus product, do not seem very useful to me.

However, it is important to think about the comparative emphasis you will put on process and product in playbuilding. It is difficult to make an absolute separation of the two because you are creating product from the very first session and the eventual performances are an essential part of the playbuilding process. But it may be useful to talk about the workshops and rehearsals as 'process' and the performances as 'product', because some directors do give inordinate time and effort to one or the other. A bad product can invalidate the most positive process by ruining the group's confidence in their voice. A good product can never make amends for a bad process because the damage of a bad process is repetitive and very deep. That damage can stifle all creative confidence in a young person.

Obviously a perfect balance between process and product would be our best aim. As this is rarely achievable, I would urge playbuilding directors to err on the side of process. If the process is positive enough, last minute energies can salvage a shaky production. If the ideas, experiences and voices of the group are respected then a positive product is always possible. If a director decides that this product must look good at all costs — and there often are these ego pressures — it is possible to bully and push kids into what passes for a slick performance. But no amount of praise to the group by audiences will heal the damage done to their creative instincts. I have seen long lasting bitterness in young people from such treatment.

On the other hand, much damage can also occur if a show is a failure. When a playbuilding show fails, the group is failing in a way that they have probably never experienced before. Playbuilding asks kids to commit their very selves to the project. Their selves are the materials for the show. They speak as themselves as well as in character. The stories told are their stories. The failure is a failure of self. If a playbuilding failure teaches a kid that his or her experience is just not good enough in a creative context, the damage can be quite devastating.

All this is a big responsibility and makes playbuilding a difficult job to handle well. From the first session all your efforts must take into account many strands of creative, learning and developmental processes, while keeping your eyes and mind fixed on achieving a product that will confirm for the group all the positive aspects of the process of playbuilding.

PRESENTING THE PLAY

The presentation of the play should fully reflect the work done and the work done should be enough to suit the presentation planned. It is damaging to the esteem and creative confidence of a group if there is a big divergence either way. While every play should have the total commitment of a group it is obvious that many plays created are fun jobs or slight exercises that would look silly if presented in a major theatre. If you have a group that thinks it is creating a bit of a sketch based on impressions of the concrete poetry movement, you must not decide at the last minute to show the piece in the school auditorium before the massed students and staff. That sort of thing is just not fair, unless the play has taken on some amazing qualities in the process. Even then, all aspects of the presentation of plays must be discussed with the groups involved. It is equally unfair to do a lot of work on a play, creating an epic, and then show it in class after school with an audience of ten.

How you decide to present a play will reflect your opinion of the work. It should be an honest reflection. It is your job as director to protect the group from over- or under-presentation. There is nothing wrong with playing to ten people as long as they are the right ten people, i.e. people to whom the play will really mean something. These comments apply to youth theatres as well as to schools. Not every play created at Shopfront will stand up to a full production season. The kids know this and respect decisions about suitable presentation. The concrete poetry play may be very effectively shown to another study group and everyone will have a good time and think their work was well worthwhile. But if the class has created a major play on violence — a topic of broad community interest — they will expect to perform the play in a good venue with reasonable audience potential.

PERFORMANCE SPACES

I talk to groups in terms of performance spaces rather than a stage, because the idea of a stage brings to mind a raised platform and certain demands for performance. Shopfront did not have a raised stage for its first five years, as a way of emphasising that theatre could happen anywhere, not just on a raised platform. My favourite space is floor-level, with the audience close. The closer an audience can get to a playbuilt show, the better the communication.

It is useful, for cast and audience, to have some way of delineating a performance space. A carpet-square can be a good method. If you use the style of keeping all the performers in view throughout the play, a carpet-square can also define when people are on or offstage. The set — often a few simple chairs or other objects — can also be placed to indicate staging perimeters. Take some care to ensure that the audience will be able to see; flat-floor seating can spoil the chance of communication. Leave enough gap between the performers and the front row for the comfort of both performers and audience. Try to provide a lot of space for the performers to work in; do not clutter the space with set and objects. Learning to focus and control energy within a large space is very beneficial to any performer. This is another way of giving the play to the performers. The space is theirs. Let them use it.

The word to remember again is 'appropriate'. A play that is having a run of four weekends may need a more elaborate set than a one-night show. A travelling play needs to be portable, of course. *The Playground Play* was toured to schools with all its props in three bags, each easily carried by one person. The team had no car and travelled to schools by public transport. Rarely is any set worth the pain of having to cart it about. Chairs are always good components of a set because almost every place you play in will have some. Chairs can be stood on too, giving a raised area for variety.

If your production is a bare one with simplicity the key-note — and this is my favourite way — it can be useful to have a few items that are really special and well-made or unusual. When we needed penguins for *Shore Sines* (and later in *Piece by Piece*) we found some lovely toy penguins that could be pushed along on sticks. Their little rubber flippers flapped on wheels as they were propelled, giving a humorous effect. The fewer props being used, the easier it is to seek out good quality items or to create special props for the show.

A youth theatre director once criticised *Childmyth* for lacking a set and told me he was into 'tinsel and glitter'. He felt this helped kids get a feel for real theatricality. I could not disagree more. It is too easy to impose your taste on the group when you have a big set and lots of props. The simpler the theatrical paraphenalia, the more strongly the play will rely on the performances of the group and on their ideas and their play.

If one of the group is specially interested in doing design work and in creating props this can be very useful. This can add an extra dimension to the work. Having someone within the group who can offer skills is always a bonus. With the design elements however, it is important to ensure that the group's designer is responsive to the ensemble nature of the work. As design can dominate a play, the design should be a true reflection of the group's work not of the taste of one individual.

SUPPORT CREW

Support crew — stage-managers; sound and lighting operators; etc — should be people who have worked with the project from the beginning, if possible. They should, in fact, have an active part in creating the play so that the work belongs to them as well as to the performers. But, in real life, it often happens that when you eventually realise that you will need a lighting operator you have to search for one. Mostly I avoid using stage-managers unless the show is a very big one. The cast gains from having to do the real work of managing their own props and costumes. I rarely use make-up people unless a show needs very special effects and even then the make-up designs will be created along with the play and the performers will do it themselves. I do not like stage make-up for ordinary playbuilt shows. Most performance situations do not really require it and make-up can easily become one of those hangovers from old-fashioned theatricals.

If you must bring in crew at the last minute, you should use young people around the same age as the performers and you should discuss with the group which people will be invited to be crew. The responsibility for the show and for discipline within the performance must remain with the group, not with a set of backstage adults conscripted at the last minute to keep order. This warning may sound terribly obvious but there seems no end to the lack of confidence adults can show in kids' abilities. Some seem to feel that young people cannot be competent without adults about. The truth is that quite often it is the emotionally disruptive and authoritarian presence of adults that throws kids into inefficiency. I have directed projects which combined kids and adults in performance and others in which adults were effective stage-managers or crew for a young group, but this was always when the adults were involved right from the beginning and naturally came to respect the kids and their work in the course of the project.

I tend to be very demanding of technical crew and stage-managers, expecting very high standards of proficiency. I point out that any mistake can make someone on stage look silly and inadequate, while the person who made the mistake is hiding safely backstage. It is very hard for a performer to work around a technical mistake whereas they can work around a performance mistake fairly readily if they have developed proper confidence. This is why I prefer to have no technical needs in the shows I direct and prefer kids to handle their own props and stage-management needs.

AUDIENCE

Choosing an audience is very similar to choosing the appropriate staging. Except for major pieces where you throw it all open to the general public, your group will probably know from the start who their audience will be. Special guests should only be invited after consultation with the group. Unless the play is strictly for lesson purposes, the group should always be allowed to invite their friends and families. Most people who have created something as special and unusual as a play like to show their work off. Their families will also want to see the work because they have probably been bombarded with stories about it for weeks.

Another good thing about knowing who your audience will be is that the play can often include in-jokes and references specific to that audience. This can be great fun for the audience, as long as you take care that no-one uses the play to be cruel. Theatre can be very effective in 'holding the mirror up' to an audience and the more specific a short-term, playbuilt show can be about its audience's lives and concerns, the more the art-form itself becomes relevant to the audience. The more relevant a group's play is to its audience, the more dynamic and appreciative their response will be.

THE DIRECTOR AND THE PERFORMANCE

While it is your job to sit at the back during the performance so that you can report honestly on the show later, you do have an important role in helping set up the show. You are the person with the expertise on theatre so you must ensure that enough preparation time is allowed. You must ensure that all aspects of the presentation have been set up and prepared thoroughly. If you are in a new space, have them check the acoustics. You should ensure that the audience arrangements are as planned, that all the support crew are there and working and that all the performers are well and in control. You should appear to be the calmest, least nervous person at the performance. This will impart two messages — that you have absolute confidence that the show will be good and that you are available to deal calmly with any personal or production problems which might arise. In some cases — when there is no stage-manager, for example — you may have to be the one who gives the cast five-minute and one-minute calls. I often choose to do this because I know that I will be sensitive and business-like about it and that's what the group needs just at that moment. They do not need someone dropping in and making silly jokes or teases just before they go on.

I do not believe in imposing on a group any formal warm-up or relaxation exercises to get them into the performance. I suggest to performers that they find some way to prepare if they need to and I insist that everyone respects each other's warm-ups or meditations or exercises, no matter how strange they may appear to be. If a group wants to do something together I encourage them to develop this amongst themselves. Many of my groups have created little 'bonding' exercises for themselves as preparation for performance. This usually only occurs when a play is to have a longish run.

If things go wrong during a performance, it is not your job to fix it. Have confidence in the group. Your interference will only make things worse. I would, of course, break this rule in case of injury to a performer, although even then I would expect the cast to deal with the matter before I realised what was going on. In *Baby Teeth* at one performance, the youngest boy in the show was actually kicked during a fight scene. A senior girl in the cast picked him up — in context — and took him to the back where he was calmed by the others. Fortunately, this is the most serious case of injury in any of the shows I have directed. There was an accidental nose-bleed in *Piece by Piece* at one performance but it occurred at such an appropriate moment that the audience thought the cast very clever to have managed such real blood. Remember that most audiences tend to think that everything that happens on stage is under control and intentional. The glaring mistakes or problems you may see are often completely unnoticed by the audience.

EXPANDING EXPOSURE POSSIBILITIES

If a group has worked hard and created something a bit better than most of us had expected at the start of the project, I like to seek out extra chances for the group to show their work. This adds just a bit more recognition of the effort and commitment they have given to the project and of the quality of the show. I do find many times that a playbuilt show, despite having been created for the moment and for relevance to a limited audience, contains such good material and surprising ideas that it deserves a wider audience. But it must be up to the group to decide if they wish to commit further to the show. It helps if extra shows can be organised to happen immediately at the end of their run so they don't have to go back into rehearsal or workshopping again. That could seem arduous just when they thought their work had ended.

Within a school you can find other classes as audience or a bigger venue or have the play videotaped. Remember that videotaping is an art-form in its own right and proper re-working of the play needs to be done to prepare it for video. The pace of a show, for instance, always seems so much slower on video than in the theatre. You may be able to have the play performed at another school or schools. You may have a youth theatre in your region who would take the production. You may have a sister-school or know of other teachers doing this work who would like to see the play. I know the problems of getting this sort of thing organised but the value to the group is enormous.

With musical shows you can arrange to tape the songs and produce a cassette. Dramatic scenes can be included as well. Recording is a job that requires discipline and effort from the group but can also give them a lot of satisfaction in the product. Audio cassettes can be good 'documentation' of your show. Shopfront has made many cassettes of their musical works and sometimes have compiled tapes representing the work of a particular year. This idea can work well in a school so that each class or drama group has an item on the cassette.

The range of interest that can be shown in playbuilt shows is almost unlimited. The work at Shopfront has been expanded beyond performances there into a wide range of extra possibilities. Shows have attracted much media interest and two major plays included in this book — *The Playground Play* and *Childmyth* — were televised nationally. These plays also became touring Theatre-in-Education shows. Plays from Shopfront have gone to festivals and on overseas tours to the U.K., Canada, the U.S.A. , France and Czechoslovakia. The early plays I did with Cleveland Boys' High were also given expanded possibilities. Some were toured to other schools; some were shown at the University of NSW School of Drama; one was videotaped by the School of Drama; *Double Cubed* was shown at a conference of English teachers and videotaped by the Drama section of the Education Department.

In most of these cases it meant doing a bit of 'selling' on behalf of the kids and you must be sure that their play is worth it. There is no point trying to push an ordinary piece of work into a high-profile situation. This can be very damaging to the group. But an extra and special performance can be an excellent reward for work well done, and a good signal to the young people that you will fight for work that excels and try to give it wider recognition.

SUMMARY

- In playbuilding, direction must be less egocentric and more collaborative than may be usual in theatre.
- Use the qualities of youth and amateurism as positive additions to the work.
- Encourage the cast to think about the performance in terms of jobs to be done on stage. This offers security, confidence and flexibility.
- Encourage the cast to go beyond the point they think they can reach, but be realistic.
- Never run performances 'by numbers'. It is their voice; they must understand what they are doing and saying.
- Playbuilding reaches for immediacy rather than greatness. Most plays will have moments of honourable failure.
- Be honest and be consistent; callous honesty is never useful. If you say something is bad, also suggest how it could be made good or suggest scrapping it.
- False encouragement is damaging. You do not help people by covering up their weaknesses.
- Set high standards for performance and give accurate praise as they approach the standard.
- When performances begin, your job is to sit up the back, make notes and watch the audience. Give notes and praise during the run to show you are doing your job.
- Carrying out tasks on stage can develop a sense of pace and rhythm.
- Don't show them how to perform; if you must demonstrate practical things make it clear that it is a demonstration not an acting lesson.
- Presentational performance should be the basic working style for all playbuilding. Declamatory and/or naturalistic acting can be included for variety and are sustainable in short bursts.
- Pace and rhythm are the icing on the cake. Don't despair if you don't get time to ice the cake; it will still be enjoyable.
- Pace and rhythm must be discussed when you reach the direction stage of the process so the cast can seek these qualities. Offer practical work in developing pace and rhythm.
- Process and product are almost inseparable elements in playbuilding. If perfect balance eludes you — and it eludes everyone — lean towards the process.
- A bad product can invalidate the most positive process by ruining the group's confidence in their voice.
- A good product can never make amends for a bad process because the damage can stifle all creative confidence in a kid.

Presenting the Play

- The presentation of the play should fully reflect the work that has been done on the play.
- Work done on a play must be enough to suit a planned presentation.
- Performance spaces are not only raised stages. Performing on the floor with audience close around seems most effective for playbuilt shows.
- Physically delineate the performance space but leave plenty of room for the cast to work in and to show their control of the space.
- If you cannot workshop the play in the performance space, ensure adequate rehearsal there.
- Keep sets, props, costumes to a minimum.
- A designer working with the group must be responsive to the ensemble nature of the work.

- Support crew should work with the group from the beginning and be involved in creating the play.
- Do not impose adult 'minders' to supervise a show; use crew of the same age as the performers if possible.
- Insist on top efficiency from all technical and support crew; their mistakes can make performers look bad on stage.
- Stage make-up is rarely useful or necessary, except for special effects.
- The director must appear to be the calmest, least nervous person at the performance. This tells the group you have confidence in them and makes you accessible to help with problems.
- The director must ensure that all necessary jobs are done in preparing for the performance.
- Warm-ups for a performance should not be imposed; let individuals or the group create their own warm-ups if they wish.
- If things go wrong during a show — except for physical injury — it is not your job to interfere; let the cast handle the problems.
- If a show is outstanding, try to offer other performance possibilities or further attention to the play, e.g. videotape it; find a more significant venue; tour to other interested groups or schools.

BABY TEETH

This project came from my suggesting the title and collecting about twenty-five kids of mixed ages — from seven to eighteen — to create the show. The name is derived from a style of print type-face and the combination of words rang bells for me in thinking about children growing up and exercising their baby teeth on the tough world. It was my last project at Shopfront after nine years as Artistic Director, which may account for the free-wheeling style and bizarre nature of the play. There is a videotape of it at Shopfront — from which the scenario has been written up — and when I came to look at it for these notes, I was a bit surprised by the play's weirdness.

That weirdness arose from the process. I have always been impressed by the wild humour that often comes from young people and I set out in this project to encourage that humour to be as bizarre as possible. This also led to a rather loose directing style in which traffic patterns and rhythm were sacrificed a little for a feeling of controlled chaos. The unusual images and ideas raised by the kids seemed to overcome the need for more formal patterns and there was a driving pace to the performances. Certainly, audiences were very entertained by it.

Our early workshops involved devising a theme for the play from that title. My idea of celebrating the growing strength of young people — 'Baby teeth can bite!' — was accepted but relegated to a fairly minor role in the play. Teeth and babies became the two principal images and scenes were created that involved these. The Dental Hygienist and the Tooth Fairy became central characters. We even got a toothpaste company and a toothbrush company to donate their products as props in the show. The kids also wanted to talk about the competitive nature of the world in which babies grow up so the play became filled with incredible contests. The contests took on a rather awful life of their own. They became a running image — a Presenter would announce one ridiculous contest after another and the contestants took each very seriously, of course.

The last comments in this play are rather like an in-joke about playbuilding. The tableau image of twenty-odd kids covered in sticky goo was quite unforgettable — especially for parents. Perhaps the message was not so clear, however, although the final false-summation ending was an attempt to remind the audience that the play was about more than the disgusting mess in tableau before them.

It is worth noting that the crazy idea of the 'custard wrestle', as we used to call it, had immense appeal to all the cast until the first rehearsal with actual custard and gunk. The dry runs had been great fun but the reality of standing about in swimmers with chocolate sauce dripping all over your hair and skin was not so welcome. The scene fulfilled the food-fight fantasies that had been expressed in creating it but became a difficult, practical job to be achieved. Despite the look of chaos, the discipline needed to carry out this scene and to hold the final tableau was a real challenge to all the cast.

Scenario for BABY TEETH

Produced by Shopfront Theatre. Created by a group of about twenty-five young participants with E. B. as director.

SETTING	We used a flat floor space with audience front-on and tiered. At the back was a raised platform for Presenters, etc. Hanging from the lighting rig on stage right was a 'tent' made from a colourful parachute. This was sometimes used as a dressing room and at other times a light inside it would be brought up to throw shadows of the performers against the tent wall when a scene was happening in there. A couple of chairs remained on the set; they were painted with big, blue eyes and 'dressed' in bootees and nappies.
INTRO	As the cast enter and take up positions, the Dental Hygienist in white coat and with clip-board delivers a speech which tells the audience, 'Tonight we

celebrate teeth' and that all the stuff on the posters about first stretching of youthful muscles is a trick to get people into the theatre so they can learn all about teeth. She says what fun people dentists are and begins reading from a dental manual.

TOOTH FAIRY   The Tooth Fairy and his Assistant interrupt. The Tooth Fairy is a tallish boy in a weird outfit of wedding dress and fur stole. His Assistant is in a sort of Superboy costume. Tooth Fairy says that he collects baby teeth and then he punches a kid in the mouth. The Assistant sweeps up the teeth with a dustpan and broom. A baby crawls across the stage and Tooth Fairy admires his teeth.

QUAD SQUAD   The Quad Squad four girls with the letters q-u-a-d on them bounce on chanting their theme song and save the baby. Quad Squad are the heroes of the play, they tell us.

(Note: The casting of people as assistants and forming squads of four helps to give everyone lots of parts when the group is very keen. However, you must ensure that each character does have something real to do.)

PETER PAN   A boy dressed in traditional green leotards, little cap, etc swings on. He has a set 'patter' which he tries on different groups of kids. 'Hi. I'm Peter Pan. I come from Never Land. I'm almost a hundred years old. Don't look it, do I? Do you want to fly back to Never Land with me? Just believe. Just believe and you can fly.' He delivers this like a salesman, several times, but each group rejects him. One girl says, 'My Mummy told me never to talk to men in green leotards.' Tinker Bell enters and tells him he's too old-fashioned for the kids. She gives him some modern accessories, including an earring and a studded leather belt. The kids mob him, thinking he is a pop-star. A girl finally recognises him and asks him to take them back to Never Land. Tinker Bell gets them into a 'magic' circle and tells them to think of something beautiful and then they'll be able to fly. Around the circle they call out their 'beautiful' thoughts — boyfriend; Mars Bar; McDonalds; pop-stars; etc. But it's not beautiful enough. Tinker Bell holds aloft a small packet of white powder and says, 'We'll have to use the magic powder'. The kids rush off-stage, following her. Peter turns to the audience and says, 'The younger generation,' and shakes his head.

(Note: The circle or line-up in which a number of alternative ideas are put forward can be a useful way to show the diversity of opinion and experience in a group. It is important that the pace of such a scene be rapid and cumulative.)

BREAKFAST SPREADS   As Peter departs, a Presenter announces the World Championship Breakfast Spread Competition. As the Presenter announces each spread a smiling 'Assistant' spreads a dab of the substance on both cheeks of a kid's face. The spread-kid says why he or she likes the breakfast spread — usually something silly like, 'I use peanut butter on my skin because it blocks up the pores and prevents pimples'. The spreads are jam, lemon-spread, Vegemite, peanut-butter and butter. The two judges are small kids who have Assistants who place sets of steps for the judges to climb up so they can reach the cheeks. They test the spreads by licking them off one cheek of each contestant.

BEING SMALL   While the licking is happening, another group comes downstage. Francine tries to get Matthew to take her out but he won't. Danielle tells her she's too young for dates but Francine is just small for her age. Several of them talk about the problems of that — being patted on the head all the time, etc — and the advantages such as getting into the movies cheap.

THE JUDGEMENT

Vegemite wins the Breakfast Spreads championship.

(Note: In this play we developed a style of scene-inserts or inter-leafing of scenes. That means doing a scene while a repetitive or drawn out action of another scene is underway. This can keep a good sense of continuous action and interest going but makes it hard to develop effective rhythm. The spreading of substances on cheeks arose when we tried to work out a practical but also interesting way to run this test. Toast was boring. In keeping with the general tenor of the play the weirdest suggestion was accepted. The various contests were structured in similar ways to weave in a pattern of ideas about competition. The competition scenes also put a lot of emphasis in this play on doing jobs rather than performing. Much of the play consisted of setting up and carrying out competitions. With such a large group this job aspect helped discipline and effective presentation.)

UNCLE DAVID READS
PETER PAN

In breathless tones, Uncle David reads two passages from *Peter Pan* to the massed kids. He reads the part about how fairies are created by the laughter of children and all the kids fall about laughing, ridiculing him. He reads how a fairy dies every time a child says, 'I don't believe in fairies.' A little girl jumps up and says that. Then she points and says, 'Look. A dead fairy'. She picks up the (invisible) fairy while all the others start yelling out that they don't believe in fairies. They find dead fairies all over the stage. They gather and ask, 'What will we do with them now?' One girl says, 'Let's have a barbecue'. They decide they have to bury them. The Tooth Fairy staggers onto the stage, dying. He falls down. The kids laugh at him. He says, 'If I die you won't get any more money for your teeth'. They decide to save him. A girl says you have to click your heels together three times but that's *'The Wizard of Oz.'* They try other formulas — abracadabra; open sesame. Finally, someone looks up the book of *'Peter Pan'* and they find they have to clap their hands, which they do. The Tooth Fairy revives. He immediately punches a kid in the mouth. This kid has a mouthful of small white lollies and staggers to the Front and spits them out. The Assistant sweeps them up. An older girl takes this boy away, telling him she can get him a nice set of false teeth through her dad. 'Look at my teeth. They're false. Aren't they nice?'

LIFETIME OF BRUSHING TEETH

The Dental Hygienist introduces a pageant of teeth through stages of life. Babies crawl about and sing a song about brushing teeth from a popular children's TV show. 'Brush your teeth, Round and round, Circle small, Gums and all.' There are actions to go with the song. The group do it as babies; teenage choir; adults shaking toothbrushes at audience sternly; old people brushing false teeth.

WORLD CHAMPIONSHIP PAIN TOLERANCE COMPETITION

Presenter announces this competition which aims to prove that young people today are just as tough as they ever were. The Tooth Fairy stomps on the kids' feet or punches them. Each screams and the screams are held around the circle, creating a chorus of screaming. Finally, Danielle holds her scream in and struggles forward, grimacing, holding it. Everyone else is silent. Tension mounts. She falls to the floor. The Presenter announces, 'The winner!' and raises her arm. She says, 'Ouch!' The Presenter calls for applause for the Tooth Fairy and as he departs all the kids throw their toothbrushes at him.

(Note: This got the toothbrushes off-stage.)

INVISIBLE FRIENDS	(In this scene all the invisible friends are played by visible people.) Mum tells Karina that she is too old at thirteen to have an invisible friend. But to Karina, Francine is quite visible. Francine is very upset that Mum can't see her. Mum 'grounds' Karina until she comes to her senses. Karina tells her younger sister, Lauren, that she shouldn't have an invisible friend. Mum pretends that Lauren's invisible friend is really there because Lauren is young. Their brother, Michael, has an invisible friend and Michael threatens that his invisible friend will beat up Lauren's invisible friend. The baby of the family wants to play with the older kids but they won't let him. He has no friends at all. The invisible friends get together to talk about their situation and Francine introduces her friend, Tilea, who is invisible to them. The invisible people tell Francine she is crazy, having an invisible friend. Mum explains the problems of the family to her husband but Karina points out that he has been dead for five years.
SIMON SAYS	A Teacher plays some games with kids, praising the goody-goody as two naughty kids — a boy and a girl — sneak away behind the tent. The Teacher plays Simon Says. She tells the class to hold their breaths and then sees the naughty kids and goes after them. The class are slowly choking to death. Someone else takes over and tells them to breathe and then do disgusting things like pick their noses. Finally she says, 'Simon says drop dead'. The class does it. The naughty kids come from behind the tent, followed by the Teacher who is staggering and has a big smile. She says, 'And don't ever do that again'.
TOUGH	One of the naughty kids says, 'Look at these wimps lying on the ground.' The group leap up and proclaim that they are tough. They chant what you do if you're tough, acting it out as they go. 'If you're tough, you smoke. If you're tough, you drink. If you're tough, you nick things from the shop. If you're tough, you bash people.' One of the older girls confronts the toughs so they decide to bash Brendan, the smallest kid. He lies crying until someone takes him away.
GRAND FINAL OF THE WORLD-WIDE INTESTINAL CAPACITY COMPETITION	(Written, more bluntly, on our scenario sheets as 'Vomit Comp.') A long speech is made in overblown prose about setting up this truly wonderful competition. 'Never before seen on stage', is said several times. The Judge is introduced. He carries a long spoon. The contest consists of people vomiting into air-sickness bags. The Judge inspects the result each time, stirring it, and tells an Assistant his verdict. Score cards for Colour, Consistency and Volume are then held up. There are about seven contestants.
'BABY FACE' STRIP	When the second contestant starts, a group of kids runs out of the tent onto the raised platform. They are in baby clothes and they all sing 'Baby Face' as they tap-dance and strip. Towards the end of the song they come down close to the audience and vamp the song up. They hold a pose for applause. During all this the vomiting has continued.
VOMIT COMP (CONTINUED)	Before the winner can be announced the Judge becomes ill and vomits into a bucket. The Presenter declares the Judge the winner.
TEACHER	Karina, the Teacher, tells her class that her stay in hospital wasn't because she had gone mad; why would she go mad with a nice class like this? Today she is going to teach them about plastic bags. She gives them all a plastic bag and tells them to put the bags over their heads. They say they don't understand and will she show them. She does and then gradually falls to the floor and chokes to death. While she is choking . . .

MINE'S BIGGER THAN YOURS	Inside the tent, the shadows of some boys can be seen. They are in a bit of a huddle. Dialogue — 'You show me yours and I'll show you mine'. 'Mine's bigger than yours'. 'Mine's got honey on it'. 'Let's get honey on ours'. The boys run out of the tent, across the stage, past the choking Teacher and go off. They all carry baby dummies. The last one stops for a moment and shows his dummy to the audience. 'See. It is big.'
TEACHER (CONTINUED)	Meanwhile the Teacher has choked to death as the kids watch impassively. The kids walk away and one girl tells the others how she had seen on television that you must never, ever put plastic bags over your head or you'll die. 'It just goes to show that television is good for you'.
GRAND SULKING COMPETITION	The Presenter introduces the competition and walks about trying to ask the Sulkers about their involvement with the sport. 'Do you think sulking should be an event in the Olympics?' No-one says much, of course. Inside the tent a boy is sulking. Danielle goes in and tries to talk to him. We see the shadow of him punching her in the eye. She staggers out and announces that he has won. The other contestants suddenly come to life, outraged by the choice. They chase the Presenter off stage.
LOVE BITES	(While the next two scenes happen out front, sheets of newspaper and a large square cloth are placed on the floor and all the equipment is set up for the wrestling scene.)
	Francine shows off her love bite. Danielle has one too. An older girl has several and boasts about all her boys. David enters and takes off his shirt to show bites all over his chest. The girl says she has bites she can't show. David meets the challenge by unzipping his jeans.
DRACULA	As David unzips, Dracula enters and conveniently flings out his cloak hiding David. Dracula is the same boy who was Peter Pan and he has a similar speech — 'Hi. I'm Dracula. I come from Transylvania. I'm more than a thousand years old. Don't look it, do I? Does anyone want to come back to Transylvania with me?' A boy volunteers. Tilea enters as a bat — she was Tinker Bell before — and says, 'I wonder what's for dessert?'
	(Note: Although some of the younger kids — such as the Peter/ Dracula boy who was ten — were not strong performers, they were able to keep full audience attention through repetition and surprise. Peter/ Dracula got a big laugh every time he said, 'Don't look it, do I?' Structuring the play so that many of the kids in their personal set of roles played inter-related characters with repeated patterns of words or movements, gave the kids a strength beyond their natural performance abilities. Concentrating the efforts of the younger ones on a limited number of jobs protected them but also gave them the chance to do well in those jobs. With this play, keeping the traffic flow precise and quick and keeping the links between scenes tight, provided a pacing that was not always sustained within the scenes themselves. The cast found it easier to deal with the jobs than to carry the longer performance periods of the play.)
WRESTLE	Bell rings. The Umpire announces a night of wrestling bouts. Dressed in wet-weather gear, the Presenter stands on the platform above the mat and describes the bouts through a megaphone as the wrestling progresses. They are called Sweets Wrestles and several bouts occur — two boys; a brother and sister; a boy and a girl; the team events. There is lots of excited shouting. The wrestlers all wear swimmers. The wrestling mostly consists of pouring gunk like custard, jams, chocolate sauces, cordials, etc all over each other.

(Note: The wrestles were well planned and rehearsed and the gunk remained confined to the mat.)

Meanwhile, at ring-side, many of the other characters of the play gather. The Dental Hygienist rambles on about how healthy it is for kids to pour this stuff over their bodies rather than over their teeth. The Tooth Fairy watches and the Quad Squad, near the end of the wrestle, leap on him, beat him to the ground and drown him by covering his face with toothpaste squeezed out of eight tubes at once. The Quad Squad try to stop the wrestle. They are all hit in the face with cream pies and the mess continues. The Dental Hygienist stands over the Tooth Fairy, holding up a tube of toothpaste. 'See, Colgate's Fluorigard Blue-Gel really does stop your teeth from falling out. Use Blue-Gel and protect your baby teeth.' On those words everyone freezes. By this time all the wrestlers are in the ring and all stand there with goo dripping off them.

THE END David and Kaela — the two oldest kids — walk forward, looking at the incredible mess, stepping over the Tooth Fairy. They walk to the front and look at the tableau. Kaela : 'Yes. But is it art?' David : 'This is the sort of play the world needs, Kaela. One with a clear message. One where you can't mistake exactly what the play is saying.' Kaela : 'Like an advertisement?' David : 'Yes, exactly. None of this arty-farty stuff. Plays of the future will be clear and simple and strong. Just like advertisements. This play Baby Teeth is a play of the future, a real trend-setter.' They say this as they slowly walk off and the lights fade.

PART TWO

PLAYBUILDING
EXTENSIONS OF
PLAYBUILDING

Territory scene, *Piece by Piece*.

CHAPTER 8

PLAYBUILDING AND SCRIPTS

Playbuilding techniques can be used in conjunction with scripts for a number of purposes. You can explore established scripts in class and workshops through improvisation and playbuilding. Writers can be helped and encouraged to write plays through playbuilding workshops. Scripts for a particular group can be written with their active participation through playbuilding workshops.

The basic working method of playbuilding — improvisation, discussion and analysis — can be applied to all sorts of creative work. Discussion sessions must follow the playbuilding fashion of being rigourous in their analysis of the work. It is easy to target improvisation sessions to specific points in a creative process or an existing script to test the processes of other work and to test improvisation results against existing results. Improvisation can be a sort of creative arts test-tube. Put a small piece of the creative work into the test-tube, swirl it about, compare results and analyse.

WRITING UP THE PLAYBUILT PLAY

I have said earlier that this should only be done if the group is very committed to it or if you can demonstrate to them a real need for a script. For example, with *The Playground Play* and *Childmyth*, we needed scripts in order to televise the work. The television director and crew could not work without a script. If the group's play is a research project you must begin with the idea of producing a final script which can be used as research reference. If the play has been very satisfying for the group certain kids may be keen to write it up for other groups to use. Being asked for the script of a play could inspire a need to write it up. However, explicit need is a significant aspect of this work. Do not establish the writing up as a tedious chore on every playbuilding project or much of the creative benefit will be lost.

If there is a good reason for writing up the play, try to ensure that as many people from the group as possible are involved in the job. It may be necessary to put the work under the control of two or three responsible people who have some writing skills. As scenes are written up they should be available to the group for checking. The checking process needs to occur as the writing happens. It is especially important to check that all important actions are included in the scripts. Often the writers will concentrate on dialogue because it is present in their consciousness but be less aware of all the actions of the play.

The director's role in the writing-up process is to ensure that an accurate and balanced script is provided. Such a script should also acknowledge that it was created through the playbuilding process so that other groups using it will have some idea of the style of work and performance needed for any production. You may have to provide the writers with some examples of how playscripts are usually presented and you may like to discuss that with the whole group. Staging diagrams and even drawings may be included to give a feel of the play's style. You have an important role in ensuring that the script belongs to the whole group just as the play did.

Do not be over-concerned about having a script of a playbuilt show. The real work and benefit has been in the process and the performances. Of all the playbuilt plays mentioned in this book, only three have been scripted. A nice shelf of scripts would sometimes be a fine thing to have, I tell myself, but not at the cost of damaging the excitement and creative benefits of the original work.

PLAYBUILDING AN ESTABLISHED SCRIPT

Playbuilding can be a very effective learning tool when applied to a play being studied in class. This is where the test-tube qualities of the process come out. It is possible to select any aspect of a script — the characters, story moments, scene linkages, visual elements — and to use one or more of these as the starting point for an improvisation. You can even develop several scenes so that a substantial body of work is available to use in creative 'testing'. By directly comparing the work created by the group with the work created in the script under study, very relevant analysis of both can occur.

If a group has done their own playbuilt show they will have a much greater awareness of the separate elements of a script and will have acquired better techniques for discussing and analysing any creative work. A group that has had a chance to improvise around the idea of penny-pinching will better understand Tyrone in *Long Day's Journey Into Night*. As director you can suggest and lead them closer to elements of the text that will help that understanding. It must be agreed between you and the group that they will let you plant bits of information that focus the work. Almost an entire play could be created about Tyrone's background, as a boy and then as a struggling actor, finally achieving fame.

The work done by the group in this way must be clearly seen by them as an exercise in approaching another person's work, not as a competition with that work. The playbuilt material will be used to illuminate and question the existing script. If the group became very keen and decided to create a whole play, let's say, based on Tyrone's early life, then the whole playbuilding process would come into force and the work would then go beyond being an exercise. Such a development must be acknowledged by all as now being in a different league and requiring a different process.

DEVELOPING WRITERS IN THE GROUP

New writers can benefit greatly from having their ideas tossed about in group discussions and in improvisations. They can also be destroyed by it if the process is insensitive. The private creations of young writers often need a great deal of tender care before being ready for group work.

Having done a lot of work with young writers I have had occasion to be able to offer them 'commissions' where the work had to be created to order rather than to their personal needs. One of these projects was a big pageant play for a youth festival. The play was to be performed outdoors in a large amphitheatre and we wanted to involve a lot of young performers. The first workshops with the young writers were much the same as first sessions for playbuilding. There were four young writers chosen to create the play — all were fourteen years old — and I worked with them as a group for several sessions before they wrote the play.

Small, the big musical.

As with playbuilding, we began by identifying the practical limitations and demands of the project. After some talk we agreed that the visual aspects of the play had to be stressed; anyone making a speech would have to use microphones; action had to be large and group action and movement should be used a lot; the play should have four segments so that each writer could use their own style; each segment should be about twenty minutes long and contain a story; the play had to be relevant to young people and on issues of 'living together', which was a theme of the festival. From this we decided to create a series of myth-like stories that could be presented in grand, bold strokes of action and language. And we called the play *Legend*.

Inspired by the festival's theme and concern with multi-culturalism, we adopted a story of different races meeting to work out a way of living together peacefully. So that these races could understand each other better, each would tell a basic legend of their race. We gave each race a colour so there were the Blue, Red, Yellow and Green Tribes. The reason for the Tribes to come together was the growing number of 'Rainbow Children' who were born of illicit liaisons between Tribes but were not acknowledged by any.

It was agreed that each writer would create the legend of one Tribe and that linking passages and all-Tribes scenes would be created by all of us in workshop. A basic motif was chosen for each Tribe — Blue Tribe was water; Red was fire; Yellow was the sun; Green the forests — and then each writer was free to create a story. When the stories were done we met again and discussed them with everyone adding ideas and helping to strengthen them. We invented a wise Black Woman to act as a link between the stories. The stories were very imaginative, making use of large design elements — a giant bird that flew to the sun; a large ship; a sea-monster — and employing dance, song and ritual. The play ended with all the Tribes agreeing to come together and a huge rainbow was held aloft by all the cast.

This was a very big theatrical undertaking. The play, *Legend*, was performed by a cast of about ninety young people from six different schools and youth groups. Each Tribe had fabulous costumes and make-up and the giant set pieces were beautifully made. A small band of young musicians provided music and sound effects. It rained on the day of the performance so the show never did happen in the amphitheatre, but it was shown the next week in the forecourt of the Sydney Opera House with an audience of some thousands seated on the steps. It was a quite wonderful setting and performance for a group of young writers to have.

Such scripts — on the large or small scale — can be developed very effectively through playbuilding processes within the script workshops, as described above. This provides the writers with a structured forum for discussion, analysis and editing of their work. It provides support and confidence to the writers through frequent assessment and discussion of the work in progress.

THE SMALL PROJECT

There are times when a group wants to work on a scripted play — to develop skills that come from this theatre work; to concentrate on production rather than creation; to work with the strengths that come from a written script; for variety. Quite often the scripts chosen for young people to perform are not at all suitable or relevant to their talents or their interests. Writing a play specifically for a group can have many of the advantages of playbuilding — working on the strengths of the group, writing for their special skills, creating relevant theatre that they can feel a commitment to, offering roles that extend each persons abilities.

Although a playwright myself, I did not write any scripts for kids until my sixth year with Shopfront. I wanted to be sure that the tradition there of playbuilding was solidly established. It is too easy for people to be creatively lazy if they think someone else will provide the material; creative busy-ness is not a normal part of most lives, unfortunately. *Small* came about because some of our younger people wanted to do a musical and because one boy was showing particular skill in performing and had expressed an interest in developing this much further. So the musical, *Small*, was written by me for a particular group and a particular performer.

The workshop sessions were similar to playbuilding. We had about three sessions before I wrote anything. These sessions were concerned with working out a story and a theme. The general theme became the idea that small is beautiful; small people — the cast — can do anything. The lead character became John Small. In order to get in all the ideas of the group we created an episodic structure that was really a series of dreams of what people wanted to be. This idea of dreams became a major theme of the play.

In the workshops we developed scenarios for each scene in quite some detail and allotted roles, so I could go away with a story-line and know who would say the dialogue. This made development of the dialogue quite easy. The songs were plotted in as well and outlines of the songs were developed in workshops. After a few weeks' break I brought back to the group the work in progress and they tried out some scenes and we edited and changed scenes as a group. The Magic Scene had to be structured around a magic act that one of the boys had devised. The Circus scene was left open for the group to develop through improvisation. A Circus Song was written to frame the scene but the circus acts and 'story' of the scene were developed in rehearsal. When the play was revived a year after its first production, the Circus scene was quite different, as it would be with every cast.

Working in this way I was able to provide specific challenges for those in the cast who wanted to develop their performance skills. But approaching the work from a playbuilding angle also provided creative input for the group and made the play specifically theirs — an exciting involvement without the final responsibility of having to 'wright' the play themselves. This project gave much greater emphasis to the production values of theatre than to the creative process. The group, although young, were experienced playbuilders and this project offered a variation and a chance to stretch their performance skills. I think a project like this can be a valuable area of drama development for playbuilders, once they have confidence in their own creativity.

Scenario for SMALL

For the second production some of these following scenes were omitted and most of the songs were shortened. The Magic Scene was dropped because there was no-one in the second cast who could do a magic routine. The production had some performers from the first season and they had a big say in the cutting of the play.

The play was staged on a floor-cloth that had the word 'small' brightly painted on it . Above the performance space a large, coloured parachute was draped. Lighting effects on the parachute gave variety and mood to the scenes. The 'orchestra' of two was on stage. Props were brought on for each scene. Lots of different costumes were a feature. A platform at the back of the stage area gave a change of levels.

The first version was in two Acts and ran for about ninety minutes. The audiences it most appealed to — under twelves — found that a bit long. In the second version we cut the play to one Act of sixty minutes and this seemed to work better with audiences. The scenario given here is of the longer version. The script is published by Shopfront. The music was written by Martin Blacker and Greg Buist.

INTRO	We meet John Small through song. His friends join him and tell us that they may be small but their dreams are big. They tell us how great John Small is and that he's their Dreamer.
JEALOUSY	Ruth and Lynne argue over John. Ruth sings the Swearing Song, but because she's not allowed to swear she has to sing 'bleep' for all the bad words.
SCIENTISTS	Small has invented a formula that will free the world from all disease. It also makes a good dog shampoo. One Scientist demands, 'But can we make it into a bomb?' They sing the Song of the Scientists which points out that their inventions are good but are sometimes put to bad use.
JUST FRIENDS	Lynne is told she's too young to fall for Small. She sings a song that says they're just friends — friends who love being together all the time and love hugging and kissing, but are still just friends.
JACK AND JILLEROO	Small, on toy horse, sings about being a Jackeroo from Walleroo who's real true blue and fair dinkum too. The cast come on as sheep and cattle and moo and baa along with the song. The Jilleroo turns out to be much more effective on the land than Small is. She can shear sheep and slaughter and cook them as well. Small dreams of having his own property one day. He asks the Jilleroo to marry him. She says, 'Don't be stupid. I'm only ten years old.'
OLYMPIC GAMES	Small is tired so they do Anne's dream of being in the Games, which end up being held in her backyard. Two Commentators tell us what is going on. The netball is cancelled because the girl who owns the ball didn't get picked in the team. They all sing a song that extols the joys of sport.
CIRCUS	Song about joining the circus is sung as the various circus acts occur. In the first production there was clowning, juggling, fire-eating, a comic knife-throwing act, tumbling, and a parade. In the second production there was clowning, juggling, a disappearing act, tumbling, a sharpshooter act, and a parade.
DREAMER	A song about how wonderful dreams can be.

INTERVAL

POP STAR	As the pop-star, Small sings a song titled 'I'm big!' At the end he is mobbed by the crowd and emerges with his clothes torn to shreds.
BOYS AND GIRLS	An argument in song about what's good about boys and girls.
AIR DISASTER	Rodney wants to be a steward. This is his dream. Kris is pilot of the jumbo and she and the stewards sing about the excitement of flying. As they do, the jet is set up on stage and a bunch of passengers enter, suitably stereotyped for a disaster. Each tells a little heart-warming story. All the cockpit crew pass out and the plane is out of control. Everyone panics. The Little Girl sings a song, 'Stand Up and Be Brave', and everyone pulls themselves together. The Nasty Kid has saved the plane by giving an antidote to the crew. He had previously given them sleeping pills. The others all throw him out of the plane which ends the dream. Rodney explains that it wasn't really a dream but an ambition.
MAGIC	Ian sings a song about doing magic and does his magic show. He explains that this isn't a dream either but his plan for what he will be when he grows up.

DREAMS AND REALITY	In song and dialogue they discuss the two concepts. Ruth says, 'There's a lot to be said for reality. At least it stays with you. Dreams float away.' The argument, in song, becomes chaotic and the musicians won't play any more. Small sings that dreams can be part of reality.
MINISTER FOR DEFENCE	Lynne's ambition is to be in parliament. The boys point out that few women get in there. Ruth is determined to be Prime Minister and threatens to beat up anyone who won't let her. Lynne is happy to be Minister for Defence and sings a snappy song about it. She sings about having wars and crushing countries, dropping bombs, but then in the chorus she explains, 'But underneath I'm such a lovely person, I watch the Muppets and Disneyland on TV.'
POLITICIANS	Ruth holds a cabinet meeting, bullying all her Ministers. Lynne wants to declare war on New Zealand. The Minister for Sport objects because this action may ruin next month's test matches. The Minister for Money says they can't afford it. Lynne suggests they could steal New Zealand's money. The most junior Minister asks, 'What if they beat us?' The war is called off.
DREAM WORLD	Small sings that he will grow up and make the whole world a dream world of peace and hope.
SUPERSMALL	Everyone is to dress up as their favourite dream character. When the others go off, Small strips off to reveal his Superman suit underneath his clothes. But everyone comes back dressed as Superman or -woman. They sing the finale — 'Supersmall'.

CHAPTER 9

FURTHER CLASSROOM OPPORTUNITIES

By now you will see the many advantages of playbuilding for developing the creativity of young people and their ability to understand and use structure in their work; for increased confidence; for honing analytical skills; for increased understanding of the creative work of others; for heightening concentration and expression skills; for broadening verbal, physical and cultural vocabulary; for understanding that achievement comes through work and that work can be fun. Many advantages from playbuilding flow into general classroom life and teachers will be able to see immediately many areas in which playbuilding projects and techniques can be applied in their classes. I am noting here just a few that have occurred for me and for colleagues who have committed time and innovation to the use of playbuilding in the classroom.

In Drama work, playbuilding offers purpose and product as well as an exciting process that can be effectively assessed by students and teachers at each step. The drama exercises and games still favoured by some teachers do not offer much substance to a class, in my view. Their purposes are usually vague and even confusing; and assessment of achievement is equally vague. Drama students want to get their hands and minds on the stuff of drama, just as pottery students want to get their hands on the clay. Playbuilding is hands-on and minds-on drama.

Teachers will also be able to see clearly how appropriate playbuilding is for any reading and writing project — in primary or secondary schools. Imagine how effective playbuilding could be in learning a language. Each character would need a vocabulary specific to his or her occupation and life-style; this would expand the vocabulary of all the class. The language would need to flow dramatically; greater fluency would result. Almost any project or subject can be developed as a playbuilding process, providing great encouragement for research and accuracy through the workshop process, play-building is a very involving way for students to learn research methods, being encouraged through the needs of the creation to check the accuracy of information with classmates and the teacher as building proceeds.

TWO-FOLD RESEARCH PROJECTS

The same topic can be playbuilt by two (or more) groups in the class, working from different perspectives. Two obvious methods would be from popular/poetic viewpoints and from straight research. For example, the French Revolution seen from a romantic and pop-knowledge view would be quite different from a play created through historical research. But the pop-play would also offer insights, as well as a comparative set of 'facts'. Why did the Revolution capture the imaginations of so many liberals and so many artists in so many different countries? Both plays could be entitled, 'Let Them Eat Cake', in order to stimulate debate. There are many such topics one could think of: the life of a writer or artist for example. A major war could be examined from the perspective of the poets of the time, from the military records, the political issues, and so on.

Bringing creative processes to learning can only be helpful, especially when those creative processes include rigourous analysis. This means that it is essential that any group applying playbuilding techniques to ordinary topics for school work must have had the opportunity to create their own play, from their own imaginations and experiences, first. They will then be familiar with the processes that arise from creative need in playbuilding and be able to transfer these readily to more scholarly playbuilding situations.

CLASS TO CLASS

It can be useful to have two classes working on the same topic and presenting their finished plays to each other. The reference material gathered would then become a research resource for both classes. Discussions after the performance would be well-informed and the students would have that familiarity with the topic which comes from really working on the material. In this case, the theme would need to be a major study topic to justify the time and attention.

With smaller topics it can be possible to have two or more classes prepare one topic each and then present their plays for discussion and as a 'lesson'. The research material would become a resource for all the classes involved in the scheme. In this way, more intensive work can be done by each group on a topic and then shared with other students. The playbuilding process and the creation of the play itself adds a passion to the study and research that is not always present in research projects at school.

VIDEO-BUILDING

It is, of course, quite possible to create videotaped dramas or documentaries using the playbuilding techniques outlined here. The same basic ground-rules apply but the rehearsal and preparation of the group for taping the show may need different skills from those required in live performance. You may need some technical experimentation to achieve a satisfactory style and pacing to the show. Video does not have the excitement and immediacy of a live performance and therefore does not produce the same emotional commitment, from cast and audience. But the medium does have its own strengths and these must be sought out and used to best effect. Video has the advantage of being a permanent record of the work.

Having such a record can be a disadvantage when it comes to working with next year's class. Why create another video when one is already there? Do not make the mistake of thinking that because video is the modern medium it will automatically be a more popular medium with young people when it comes to creating drama. I have noticed over a period of years that most entrants in a national young writers project have chosen to submit scripts for the stage. Why didn't all these young TV-watchers write drama for TV, the medium with which they were most familiar? I was even more intrigued to find that many kids who were writing stage plays had seen very few professional shows. So why did they write for the stage? The general answer I got could be summed up by saying that they

Kids Kabaret. A musical compilation show.

felt TV was for 'entertainment' but that a writer who really wanted to say something important had to write for the theatre.

COMPILATION PLAYS

What I call 'Compilation Plays' are similar to documentaries and they are a very effective format for study projects, as well as for special events. At Shopfront these sorts of plays were used when celebrating a fifth or tenth anniversary, or when touring a play that showed the work done over a period of time. A school can compile a play about its history and work in that way too, but for classroom work, the Compilation Play offers a method of thorough study of material with an imaginative result. A play must be limited in time, so a selection of material is necessary and the topic must be looked at in detail before that selection can be made. A group quickly finds that the more they know about a subject the more interesting, surprising and substantial their play will be.

A good example of this technique is The Shakespeare Show which I created with a Theatre-in-Education team at Shopfront. The play set out to introduce students to the work of Shakespeare in performance. We chose material that could be presented in an entertaining way and deliberately chose staging styles that were varied and interspersed with tricks, songs and surprises. One aim was to show that Shakespeare could be relevant to modern life. The compilation of the show took a lot of research and experiment with extracts from the plays, songs and poems of Shakespeare.

The show was created and performed by four young men: Kingston Anderson; Greg Bull; Michael Curnick; Terry Ryan. They acted as a troupe of Elizabethan strolling players who had one big box with them, out of which came their stage setting and costumes. The costumes were in full sight and quick changes occurred behind the small set. The play was introduced to the ringing of bells. 'We have selected for your entertainment the most intellectually stimulating segments from the works of Will Shakespeare. See Macbeth beheaded. See Julius Caesar assassinated. See Brutus commit suicide. See Hamlet's family poisoned and stabbed. See Polonius stabbed. See Tybalt stabbed. This is a show for the whole family.'

This element of a world of violence portrayed in the plays was one continuing theme of our show. The fight between Prince Hal and Hotspur was done with lots of power, using two-handed swords made from steel bars. The fight between Tybalt and Romeo was done in classic swordfight style with furniture knocked over and actors rolling about. It looked quite wild.

An ongoing linking device was an Interviewer from the EBC — the Elizabethan Broadcasting Corporation — who was able to introduce segments so that the audience would have some background to the play they were seeing and the segment could make sense out of context. He wore a T-shirt labelled EBC and Shakespeare wore a T-shirt with his face drawn on it and the word 'Bill'. The first interview with Bill was about his life and all the answers were quotes from his plays. As he answered, a Fool stood on a chair and held up a bright handkerchief on which the name of the play being quoted from was written.

The Interviewer told Bill that he was a great fan and especially liked *Hamlet*. Bill said, 'An ill-favoured thing, sir, but mine own'. The *As You Like It* handkerchief was displayed. Of Bill's hard life as a glove-seller, he said, 'My friends were poor but honest' (*All's Well That Ends Well*). 'If I chance to talk a little wild, forgive me. I had it from my father' (*Henry VIII*). When Bill is accused of being disenchanted with life, he says, 'It is a tale told by an idiot, full of sound and fury, signifying nothing' (*Macbeth*). And his new-found success? 'The world's mine oyster' (*Merry Wives of Windsor*). Sometimes the Fool was hard-pressed to keep up with the fast flow of quotes.

Another continuing thread of the show was the use of scenes from *Romeo and Zelda* which Bill admitted did not sound quite right. He suggested *Aaron and Zelda* but also insisted that he never re-wrote anything in his plays, 'In five hundred years people will still speak of the love story of Romeo and Zelda.' The use of boys to play the female roles was explained at this point and we rarely got a laugh when the burliest young man in the troupe appeared on the balcony as Zelda. This point was also dealt with by Shakespeare reciting one of his love sonnets to the Interviewer, looking deep into his eyes. The Interviewer assured Bill that he and his girlfriend often read them to each other.

Yet another continuing device was a 'countdown' of Bill's Top Ten Speeches. These were recited throughout, with 'Once more unto the breach' coming in at number two and 'All the world's a stage', at number one. The play was begun by each performer making a major speech and was ended by each giving an Epilogue. The very last speech — not really an Epilogue — was 'Our revels now are ended' and as it was said everything was packed up and put back in the box, which was all that remained on the stage.

Songs were used throughout the show. Some were from Shakespeare's plays and others were associated in some way, e.g. a snatch of song from *West Side Story* and 'Brush Up Your Shakespeare'. A long segment — some ten minutes — from one of five plays being studied in schools could be selected by teachers as the second-last scene, before the Epilogues. In this way we prevented the show from becoming too fragmented. There was material used from twenty-three plays and two sonnets, so a decent slab of drama at the end was a necessary piece of substance.

The amount of research to produce this Compilation Play was considerable. Sometimes what we thought we knew about Shakespeare and his plays was wrong or ill-remembered and much brushing up of our own Shakespeare knowledge was needed. That was one of the great benefits to us as a T.I.E. team that can also accrue to a class or group of young people when they embark on a Compilation Play. The type of imagination and fun that went into The Shakespeare Show can be applied to many different topics. The need to use the research material to entertain an audience — and you must insist that the plays be entertaining, not lectures called plays — will make the research come alive for the creators of the play in a way that few other research and learning methods can.

THE ROMANCE PROJECT

This was a broad-based, creative project done with a class at J.J. Cahill High with English teacher, Wendy Perry. The class was made up of thirty girls and boys, all about fourteen years old. There was reluctance in the class to study *Romeo and Juliet* so we decided to approach the subject of romance from many different angles with each group asked to create some finished product on the topic. Some chose to do this through photography; some through a study of teenage magazines and romance novels; some created a videotape about love, through playbuilding.

After some success with the early video-building sessions, we persuaded most of the class to be involved in a video of *Romeo and Juliet* to be set in the school and using students of different races to portray the lovers. The students were able to relate to that idea quite easily — a Chinese girl and an Anglo-Saxon boy being forbidden to see each other was within their experience. Gangs hanging out in the playground; a knife-fight at lunch-time; drugs for sleeping draught and poison; a Headmaster instead of the Prince; were all dramatic elements that the group could relate to. We used little dialogue so that they did not have to learn lines and we over-dubbed speeches later. The balcony scene became Romeo's thoughts as he watched Juliet going up the steps into class. The knife-fight was shot from above from a classroom window and the whole school yelled encouragement from other windows. Romeo's body was carried out of the woodwork rooms. The gymnasium became the scene for the secret marriage of the lovers. The Nurse became a bossy teacher and the Friar was now a friendly teacher. As Romeo's body was borne from the school, the Headmaster's voice intoned the last speech, 'Never was a story of more woe than this of Juliet and her Romeo'.

Such a treatment of the play is not sufficient on its own of course, but this project did open the doors wide for fuller study of the play. When the edited video was seen by the class they were involved in their own acting-out of a Shakespeare play and they were listening to their own voices saying the poetry. Despite their early reluctance, their coming to grips with the drama in an active way made the play more alive and compelling for them.

The other work in this project became more significant as the video of *Romeo and Juliet* progressed. Even those who thought they had chosen an easy option began to see direct connections between what they were doing on the project and the 'school work'. The playbuilt video, called *Different Loves*, was set in a coffee shop where clandestine love affairs abounded. Some of these were quite funny and clearly influenced by TV. But others dealt with serious issues such as loneliness, homosexuality and love between people of very different ages. These topics were looked at sensitively and provoked a lot of discussion amongst the group.

Within the overall project it was clear that the drama-based work involved the class in a much more dynamic way than the other research and photography options. In trying to be terribly democratic about the work we may have denied some students the chance to step more fully into the drama, although everyone in the class did play some part in the *Romeo and Juliet* tape. The excitement of the work certainly spread about the school. Teachers helped with adult voices for the tape but were also disconcerted that students wanted to take over rooms in recess and lunch breaks for rehearsals and preparation of work. Perhaps our planning was a bit chaotic and some people were not quite ready for it. But then we had not expected it to spill over so energetically into the general life of the school. The amount of effort put into this project by most of the students was quite inspiring.

FURTHER DEVELOPMENT
FOR A GROUP

Playbuilding can go on being a very satisfying activity for a group for years. Each play provides new challenges and each play done by a young person provides development of creative abilities and skills. The playbuilding process often prompts young people to look for specific development, sometimes in performance areas; sometimes towards writing; sometimes in particular topics or theatrical styles. There are also educational needs that call for planned development in drama studies. The question arises sometimes of where to go next.

HARDER PLAYBUILDING

A group or class should be led into more difficult challenges each time they embark on a playbuilding project. The director must make greater demands for innovation, precision, thorough research, clear analysis and skilled performance. When a group has been through two or three playbuilding projects they should be an effective team of creative and flexible thinkers and performers. The playbuilding process can then become more specific in looking at strands of drama that demand greater effort and thought.

The Character Play is a good development for a group. Character is seldom dealt with in any depth in Theme Plays. Work on character needs to be sensitive and will demand that the group take some emotional risks in the process. With a background of playbuilding projects behind them, kids do not feel so reluctant to venture into risky areas. These areas make greater demands on the director as well and you must be very careful to give full protection to your group. Your intuition and sensitivity will have to be on the alert. Your demands for ever deeper exploration into character will have to be persistent but sensitive.

Story Plays, Setting Plays and Compilation Plays can also be used to lead groups into detailed work in a particular strand of drama. These projects can be used to emphasise specific skills and areas of creativity and all of them will also — along with work on Character Plays — help greatly in the general ability of the group to playbuild and to bring the playbuilding process to their other creative work and studies. A Story Play project will hone areas of structuring ability that may not have been stretched in other playbuilding. Compilation projects emphasise breadth of research and careful selection of research results to dramatic purposes. Setting Plays can offer work on sustaining mood and atmosphere in more intense ways than in most other playbuilding.

PRODUCING PRESENTATIONAL SCRIPTS

A development in the direction of greater emphasis on performance skills and theatre study is to produce a scripted play. The step is more natural and beneficial if the play chosen is of the presentational type. Classical Greek theatre and Shakespeare are presentational plays, as well as Brecht and Epic Theatre, and are excellent areas of extension of playbuilding skills. I have noted before that presentational acting is related to the way we all 'act' in real life and a class or group can be readily accommodated into a presentational production; whereas many will not have the skills or style needed for plays that require naturalistic or realistic acting. Certainly, a production of a naturalistic play with content relevant to young people can be a developmental exercise for some in a class. But the big majority of young people will respond more positively to the demands of a play that is presentational in style.

The choice of play to be produced is of utmost importance. It must offer a story or theme that young people can relate to. It will usually be the director's job to choose the play and to sell it to the group. There are many that offer rich opportunities for performance development and also for analysis and discussion of the issues raised. The play should be chosen to engage mind, heart and body, just as you would expect to do in a play-building project. If possible, select a play that has some significant place in theatre history. This brings the work of the group into contact with important theatre that can be studied and relished.

I also think it is vital to offer the group a director's interpretation of an established play. This will correspond in some ways with the voice that they have in playbuilding and, of course, you should make the interpretation one that is open to discussion and input from the group. Discussion and analysis then is engaged on the history of the play and the interpretation as well as on the issues raised in the play. The interpretation should be one that offers a topical perspective on the play, if possible. Dealing with classic plays can also give you the great advantage of being able to adapt the play, even impose on it a contentious view, which then provides much food for discussion and study.

Shakespeare deserves a section of his own and this appears below. But there is quite a rich field of presentational and classic works to choose from. I will mention two here that I have produced with young people. One was modern and one ancient. The modern play was *Andorra* by Max Frisch. This is a very strong play about racial and religious prejudice, set in a fictional country called Andorra. A young man is persecuted for being a Jew to appease Andorra's racist neighbour. Finally he is handed over to the soldiers of the neighbour, thus protecting Andorra from invasion. The boy, Andri, comes to believe he is Jewish, because of the way he is treated, even though his father tells him the truth. Andri is an illegitimate son but the father had been too ashamed to admit his infidelity, so told everyone that the boy was a Jewish refugee rescued by the father. The issues of the play are very complex and quite harrowing, but they are presented in strong, simple images.

The two aspects of the play that I stressed for production were the characterisations and the design. Most of the characters were stereotypes and were dressed in white shirts with the relevant title printed on each — 'Soldier'; 'Priest'; 'Teacher'. This clearly placed the performance style as presentational and was also useful to the audience with a cast that was aged from early to late teens. The design was created by a brilliant young designer, Michael Hill, who was fourteen at the time. He used large wooden packing-crate panels painted in bright colours with stylised picture-postcard images on them to suggest that Andorra was a quaint, jolly country. There was a sign that said, 'Welcome to Andorra.' There were birds made from wood and leather, hanging over the scene. This 'pretty' vision of Andorra clashed with the solid, unyielding materials that the set was made from, and provided the right atmosphere for the play.

Michael Curnick as Caliban, *The Tempest*   Nick Carlile as Ariel, Gerry Tacovsky as Ferdinand,
The Tempest

The play offered the cast a central character near to their own ages and an issue that is timeless. The relevance of the play and the style of the production enabled us to focus discussion on the issues as well as on performance demands. This made the experience important and developmental for the group.

The second play was *Orestes* by Euripides, which I directed with a mixed aged group. The issues were very significant and the ending — with its overtones of terrorism — was particularly relevant at the time. We concentrated quite a bit on the theatre history of the piece, researching costuming and masks and discussing at length the Chorus role in the play. A lot of work was done to develop dances for the Chorus and to create music for the show. Our masks were not of classic style but made from the faces of the cast. We built a small, classic stage with walkway above for the final scenes and the appearance of Apollo — played by a local apprentice butcher. We nailed dozens of masks all over the walls of the stage. The oratorical nature of the play was presented by use of microphones at the edge of the stage. Occasionally a speech would be made directly into a microphone.

The cast responded strongly to the story, again a harrowing one, and to the issues. They particularly liked the cynical way in which Euripides deals with the beauty, Helen, and the hero, Menelaus. The last violent image appealed also for sheer relevance as well as theatricality. Orestes holds his sword at the hostage's throat and the three young people prepare to burn the family home, while Menelaus and his army fume helplessly below. It was like something on the television news. The outrageously silly appearance then of Apollo to solve all the problems also gave us a great deal to discuss about theatrical imagery and its power to comment.

After the season finished, we all met with some parents and other audience members to discuss the project of *Orestes*. The discussion lasted some hours and we concluded that the project had been something of a disappointment. We had set many goals of research and performance development that had not been fully realised. We had identified a number of performance problems but had not solved them satisfactorily. The elements of dance, music, mask and oratory had not been integrated into the production effectively enough. But our conclusions showed a great honesty on the part of the group about their work and a willingness to analyse the work in detail.

The audience members in the discussion objected to our self-criticisms as being too harsh. They said how fascinating they had found the show to watch, despite some problems. Surely, they told us, a show cannot be bad if it provides an interesting night of theatre for its audience. The argument is a reasonable one but theatre with young people has other criteria that must be given weight. Audiences for theatre by young people will often be pleased just to see their kids on stage or will be impressed that the kids 'remembered all the words'. Directors and casts have to be more critically aware than this. Our judgement on *Orestes* was not a negative action because we were busily noting all the areas that must get special attention next time we did a play like this. We also acknowledged in the discussion the achievements and the pleasure that we had gained from the experience. But playbuilding process demands that real assessment be made of the work so that lessons can be learned and growth continue.

SHAKESPEARE

My own school years turned me off Shakespeare almost totally. As a child I was always amazed that his writing had fooled so many people for so many years. Boring, irrelevant and unintelligible, that was my 'educated' judgement. Today this sort of experience is still common. Yet young people can really enjoy Shakespeare and can relate very strongly to his work. There are two main reasons why I now choose to do Shakespeare so often with young people — he is almost always being studied; and kids should be encouraged to work on the best material available. Shakespeare certainly provides rich fields of theatre to till.

As well as producing the Compilation Play, *The Shakespeare Show*, I have been involved in productions of *Othello* (not very successful at all); *Hamlet* (an interesting experiment); *Romeo and Juliet* (exciting); *The Tempest* (very effective and also played as T.I.E. show in school); *A Midsummer Night's Dream* (very successful); and *As You Like It* (with an all-male cast, very entertaining and successful).

The lack of success of *Othello* was mostly due to inexperience on the part of everyone involved, especially myself, and to the lack of relevance the play had to the students' lives. It was done only because it was on the syllabus, so it was a rather mechanical exercise, on reflection. With the other productions I went to some trouble to involve the casts in the issues of the plays and to select plays that offered something special to each group. All the other productions also offered real interpretations of the plays and, except for *A Midsummer Night's Dream*, were adapted to suit the needs and skills of the performers.

With *Romeo and Juliet* I worked on the adaptation. The production was directed by a colleague at Shopfront, Kingston Anderson. He decided to place the play in Belfast, using modern dress and slides of the Belfast conflict in between scenes. The script was not changed at all until the cast had done a rehearsed reading of the play. At that point we all discussed the way the show was shaping and realised that there were problems with the interpretation and also with the cast's varying abilities with the long speeches. These speeches also tended to slow the action of the play which Kingston had imagined as quite hectic, in keeping with the Belfast motif. After much discussion I adapted the play to a much shorter version.

I have adapted several Shakespeare plays now and have drawn up certain guidelines. It is imperative to retain the rhythm of the lines and the rich use of language and imagery. Given the modern tendency to dislike oratory I try to reduce those speeches first, but always cut so that rhythm is retained. I do very little updating of language because part of the joy of doing Shakespeare is to look at the richness and history of the language and because too much word changing will damage the poetry. I do change 'thee', 'thou' and 'thy' so that the usage can flow more readily and feel a touch more modern. Such changes can make a play tighter, shorter and more accessible to the young cast and to a youth theatre audience. Let's not pretend to offer definitive versions of the Bard in these productions. Adapting Shakespeare for young people to perform provides an important way of introducing them to great writing and great theatre.

Probably the most important thing I do when adapting Shakespeare is to type the plays out as if they are prose. This enables young people to read and speak the lines clearly right from the start of rehearsals. They do not have that awkward line-ending to baulk at. I find that this little trick also helps them to speak the lines poetically because they concentrate on where the language is leading them rather than on the layout of the lines.

With *Romeo and Juliet* the shortened version helped the cast into the play and into the interpretation that Kingston had devised. He broadened the approach so that the slides shown between scenes were from many conflicts, particularly where religious differences were the basis and where young people were involved. This device added a grimness to the production that was very modern and relevant and gave an urgency to the action as well. The set was stark white and the costumes were 'old-fashioned, timeless', which fitted with the language of the play but did not distract from the modernity of the issues. Kingston also added a rather brilliant touch at the end. When the Prince came forward to make his last speech, a 'terrorist' in a ski-mask ran forward and shot him. The Prince fell back into the arms of the Capulets and Montagues and that moment was held as the lights faded. This gave the play a sharp jolt into the modern age and into modern cynicism; an ending highly approved of by the cast.

The first big 'classic' that we did at Shopfront was a version of *Hamlet* adapted by me into a version called *Hamlet, 16*. The young people wanted to do a major script and the staff felt that it would be good to keep kids who were busy creating their own plays in touch with the history of Western theatre. This led, in fact, to the production of a 'classic' each year for some years. I did a lot more fiddling about with *Hamlet* than I should have and much more than I have ever done since with any Shakespeare. The basic premise of our version was that Hamlet should be presented as a sixteen-year-old, not mature enough to take over the crown. I have always felt that the play would make much more sense if Hamlet were seen as being that age, given his behaviour and his attitude towards his mother and uncle. So all Hamlet's friends were to be around sixteen too. The Gravediggers were apprentices — I gave them some lines about the master not getting out of bed in the middle of the night. Fortinbras was the same age as Hamlet, which provoked Hamlet's jealousy. We also decided that adult roles should be played by adults — this also happened in *Romeo and Juliet* — and involved parents in the roles of Claudius, Gertrude, Polonius and the Leader of the Players, who were a children's troup — popular in Shakespeare's day. The age range of the cast was from seven to fifty-five.

Although rather immodest about adding scenes to *Hamlet*, I did it with a definite interpretation in mind that was designed to stir up some of people's expectations about the play. The piece performed by the Players, for example, was a brief version of *Orestes* (*Hamlet* is labelled by some critics as an Orestes-myth play). The boy who played Orestes was dressed as Hamlet, so that Gertrude also had a 'recognition' moment during the play-within-a-play, which led into the intense scene between mother and son. This scene was quite electric when played between a teenage Hamlet and a middle-aged Gertrude.

Although I would now be totally reluctant to write new scenes for Shakespeare, the basis of the *Hamlet, 16* experiment was sound and had good results. The cast felt involved in the modern psychology that our version stressed and were caught up in the historical study that also underpinned the interpretation. The performances created much discussion and led to continuing productions of the classics at Shopfront.

A Midsummer Night's Dream was a more straightforward production of the play. A little cutting was done on the script. The main angle of interpretation was to emphasise the reality of the fairy world and the unreality and falseness of the world of the court. The court characters mostly wore masks. The lovers did not and were the link between the dreams and the reality. With a very large cast available we were able to incorporate a lot of singing and movement that added to the dream quality of the show. We often used the effect of having the fairies watch the action of the humans. All the fairies came out to watch 'Pyramus and Thisbe'. We also composed our own music for the show and played it live.

Having read about all-male productions of *As You Like It*, I was intrigued to try the idea.

Certainly, in reading the play, it is very clear that Shakespeare wrote many of the jokes and humorous situations around the fact that his women were played by boys. This is especially so of the scenes between Rosalind and Orlando where Rosalind is disguised as a boy who teaches Orlando about love by pretending to be Rosalind. Much of the humour of these scenes relies on having a boy play Rosalind.

We produced *As You Like It* in presentational style so that the boys who played girls did not have to be 'girlish' at all. They presented the lines and the situations strongly and the characters came through that. Although the convention of boys playing girls is not common on modern stages, our audiences had no problems in relating to the style and did, I think, find all the cross-sexual fun that Shakespeare wrote into the text.

This production was presented with an all-female production of *Lysistrata* by Aristophanes, directed by Faye Westwood. Both plays had to be cut to fit the double-bill. The Greek play also worked well as a one-sex production and the broad, stylised characterisations that the girls presented suited the script and interpretation so that, again, audiences accepted the convention quite happily.

The Tempest was probably the most successful and interesting adaptation I have done of a Shakespeare play. It was prepared for performances in schools by the Shopfront Caravan — a T.I.E. team with eleven members — and also had some in-theatre seasons. The touring nature of the show put some boundaries on our interpretation as did the cast limitation of eleven. There were three young women in the team and two of them played male roles — Trinculo and Stephano. To keep the play within reasonable time limits some segments were cut. The masque scene was omitted and Prospero's wonderful speech, 'Our revels now are ended', was transformed into a song to finish the play. That song was sung by all the cast with music played by five guitars, drums, triangle, tin whistle and cymbals. It was an extremely stirring moment.

Music was a very important element of the production. We decided to write all our own, rather than use music that existed for the actual songs in the play, because we were turning some of the dialogue into songs and wanted a sense of wholeness to the musical aspects of the show. Again, the amazing Martin Blacker created the music. Music provided a unifying thread of interpretation and highlighted the very poetic nature of the language and themes of the play. Prospero and Ariel used instruments such as drums and cymbals to create some of their magical effects. Various cast members became musicians at different times in the show. With so many cast members able to play instruments and with many good singing voices in the cast, the music emphasis was certainly a way of working on the strengths of the cast.

Because the cast were all young we also emphasised the presentational style of acting. There were two methods of doing this. Firstly, we used stylised make-up on all characters. Secondly, all performers remained on stage throughout the play and simply stepped forward when their entrances were due. These elements were helped along by a number of other devices — the music and dance; the on-stage 'orchestra' space with drums on wooden frames providing an imaginary line between on and off stage; the beginning of the play with the actors preparing on stage, putting final touches to make-up as the audience came in; a mirror on-stage that actors used to check costumes and make-up during the play; women in male roles; 'old-fashioned timeless' costuming; open-stage and virtually no set — a couple of wooden chairs and wooden logs were used as furniture.

The make-up effect was quite interesting. Most wore a full-face smear of white, similar to light white-face clown make-up. Prospero had large, coloured diamonds on his face — a rather wizard-like effect. Caliban's make-up was like military camouflage in greens and browns. Ariel's face was bright yellow with cheekbone highlights in red. Gonzalo had black lines under his eyes to suggest age. The costumes were very simple but each wore something to indicate their station in life and their position in the play. Ariel was bare-chested and wore an exotic scarf of bright blue with heavy silver thread through it. He used this to induce spells and set up barriers.

The text was shortened and some characters omitted. The major change was the omission of the masque scene, which diminishes the magic element of the play perhaps but allows more pace and more emphasis on the story. We also omitted the magic banquet offered to the King and his followers. The effect of the shorter, less 'magic' version was to place more responsibility on Prospero's humanity in his treatment of the ship-wrecked people on his island. This aspect was also highlighted in our interpretation of the relationship between Prospero and Ariel. We showed Ariel as near-human in many ways and so he became quite emotionally involved with Prospero and with his plans for vengeance. This is especially borne out in the scene where Ariel pleads for Prospero's victims: 'If you now beheld them, your affections would become tender . . . Mine would, sir, were I human.' Prospero accepts this chiding and becomes more 'human'. This interpretation tended to portray Prospero, Ariel and Caliban as three aspects of humanity working out a balance inside the story.

Turning some longer speeches into songs was a very useful device that added to the poetry and overcame some of the problems of performing long speeches. This also made the speeches more acceptable to young audiences. An example of this was Ariel's speech, describing the storm. Starting with, 'I boarded the king's ship', and finishing with, 'Hell is empty, and all the devils are here' — which was repeated and sung by all the cast — Ariel sang the speech, pushing the excitement of the story to the strong musical beat. In other cases we had the whole cast sing songs allocated to Ariel in the script — 'Come unto these yellow sands' and 'Full fathom five' — to heighten the presentational style of the show and to heighten mood. The music was not rock, but it was all played on instruments, mostly guitars, that young audiences could relate to readily. Nothing in the style of the show was out of the imaginative reach of young audiences and so the show was able to carry the poetry and Shakespeare to their imaginations.

In leading young people into productions of plays, the idea of keeping the work within their reach is important. This is achieved by your approach to the production, not by the cleverness or originality of your ideas. A device used within the Shopfront *Tempest* would be perceived as within reach because the group understood the many elements that went into such an effect. The same device in an Australian Opera production at the Opera House would probably be perceived as being beyond their reach. It is vital that young people have many opportunities to touch, feel, use and appreciate theatre for themselves, both as participants and audience, so that they discover that there is no theatre that is really beyond their reach, so that they discover that all the richness, drama and poetry of all theatre is accessible to them.

PART THREE

TWO SPECIAL PLAYBUILDING PROJECTS

Ned Kelly scene, *Dancing with Kangaroos*.

CHAPTER 11

PIECE BY PIECE AND DANCING WITH KANGAROOS

The two plays detailed in this chapter are especially exciting and useful examples of playbuilding processes and products. Both were created for overseas tours and both were acclaimed by audiences, teachers and theatre professionals as outstanding products. But the processes by which these plays were created were very different. For *Piece by Piece* (PxP) the process was quite rapid, intense, almost problem-free and very satisfying for all of us. This led to a play that was based in language and in detailed thought about the theme and about each idea raised. *Dancing With Kangaroos* (DWK) had a drawn out process, full of dead ends. The group were often unhappy with progress and negative about the play's potential. Almost every scene caused argument within the group rather than discussion. The whole process was unsettling for all of us. This led to a play that was based in deep emotional revelations about the group's relationship with Australia, shown through stylised scenes, much silent movement and creation of striking visual symbols and effects.

Despite the very different processes — caused partly by the very different composition of each group — both projects created outstanding products. I believe this was because I managed to adhere to the basic principles of playbuilding, despite many mistakes and a lengthy false start with DWK, and insisted on rigorous attention and examination of every aspect of the creation of a scene before adding any element. Because the PxP group were experienced in playbuilding, they recognised this process and the fast progress we made. It was also easier to explain it to them because the progress was verbal and responded to verbal explanation. The DWK cast were generally inexperienced in playbuilding and did not easily recognise progress. It was a problem inherent in the style we had chosen that much of its impact was visual and emotional. But, with DWK, it was enough that I could see and feel the progress because the group had no choice but to trust me until they were able to feel the results themselves. Part of our difficulty as a group was that the cast had no satisfaction from the project until we had actually performed the play and found it worked. My big limitation lay in my inability to explain the process to them. There is no doubt that the PxP project was the easier one to achieve.

Both had one aim in common — to create a play that could be shown to overseas audiences and remain Australian without being too limited. This aim created lots of pressure, of course. Would people understand what a bunch of young Australians had to say? Would anyone care? Could kids make a play that was good enough? As Shopfront had done tours before some of these questions could be given positive answers, but pressure was still there to see if these particular groups could do it too. The PxP cast included three very strong playbuilders who had toured overseas before. The DWK cast had done very little playbuilding and had never toured. The PxP cast were creating a play about peace for a Festival. All of them were intelligent kids who had ideas on peace and the play's process was simply to test and shape those ideas into theatre. The DWK group were trying to say something revealing about their country — a very difficult task. How do you find the essence of Australia? Most young people respond by saying it's the greatest place on earth with good beaches and great weather. But this group wanted to be critical and to find why we love the place. We wanted to show audiences a relationship — a relationship between these twelve young people and their country. Very difficult to do, and the emotional stresses were considerable.

Many of the boundaries for the PxP project were established from outside Shopfront. Our invitation to an International Youth Festival in Vancouver — and the airfares provided — stipulated that the group consist of eight young performers and two staff. The play had to be up to fifty minutes long and very portable so that performance areas could be effectively scheduled. The play could be on a choice of three themes of which we felt Peace was the most interesting. Given that the play would be in competition with youth theatre groups from many countries and with professional groups performing for youth audiences, we decided to concentrate on creating a very verbal play as that was our real strength and we wanted the best play we could achieve for such an international event.

The speed and efficiency with which PxP was created resulted directly from the selection of cast. Most had been at Shopfront for years and had a great deal of playbuilding experience. While this is unusual in such a young group, you will find in any group or classroom young people with a range of abilities and approaches that can be harnessed for strong, creative teamwork.

False ego demands are usually the blocking factors in groups of playbuilders. The PxP group knew from experience that the best favour you can do your ego is to put it to work for the group. There was a sort of shorthand language within the group that led to great progress being made on almost an hourly basis.

Such progress is to be expected, of course, if what I have been saying about playbuilding in this book is true. Consider the PxP group. I had worked with Liz for eight and a half years; with Martin for over six years; and with Francine and David for five years. Of the others, three had not been in a playbuilding project before but brought outstanding performance skills. All the group made full and open contributions to the playbuilding process. Such a happy coincidence of experience and abilities, combined with the excitement of the project, gave us a close to perfect playbuilding process.

However, it is fair to say that we, as a group, did not achieve the sort of rich emotional resonance and personal national revelation that was so admirably reached by the 'imperfect' team assembled for DWK. In some ways, the DWK team was much braver because they were asked to go further, emotionally, and they stuck at that challenge through a stormy process. I raise this point not to award medals but to demonstrate that the level of achievement is often dictated by the goals set in the early sessions. The PxP team went further than was demanded of them and delivered a well-crafted, deeply-considered, deeply-felt play that stirred all who saw it. They were not asked to bare their souls; they were asked to find intelligent words and images to express their passionate desire and need for peace. How do you say, 'We want peace' in new and exciting ways? That is hard, but the PxP team did it wonderfully well — and through a model playbuilding process.

The DWK team were asked to show what Australia is; what the soul of Australia is. That is impossible, but this group, staggering about through a strangely chaotic and aggressive process, almost achieved it and certainly achieved a play that entertained but also unsettled its audiences. I am encouraged by these two projects to think that young people can tackle any project through playbuilding and achieve high levels of success, if their director stays true to the original goals and insists on choosing the rigourous options rather than the easy ones.

When the first performance of DWK occurred, all the pieces fell into place in a remarkably polished and poetic performance. This occurred just two weeks after the first rehearsal of the full play when we were still in despair about whether it could ever work. The first show was played to a school audience of teenagers who were confronted and, in some cases, affronted by the images they saw, because they recognised them so clearly and recognised what the group were showing underneath the images. These levels of recognition and the suddenly successful play-structure occurred because each piece of work had been tested, tried, fought over and carefully placed, even when we, as a group, did not have a clear vision of the final product. DWK was a real testimony to the strength of the playbuilding process — even when flying blind. It was rather fitting then that this group not only had great success with their play overseas, but also did a very successful playbuilding demonstration workshop with me for an audience of professional theatre people in Prague.

PIECE BY PIECE

Early in the project the group decided that the theme of peace should be explored from a personal perspective as well as globally. It was not to be an anti-nuclear play but a full peace play. This led to a fairly straightforward message for the play: find peace within yourself and then gradually spread that to your family, friends and the world. The play showed how hard it was to achieve any of those things but did always try to suggest hope.

In *Shore Sines*, three of the group had already helped create a significant and popular scene about peace: 'The Ballad of the Penguin and the Lion'. After some discussion we decided to include it in this play and we also decided to include the song, 'Tomorrow and Tomorrow and Tomorrow' — words by Shakespeare and music by Martin Blacker. This gave us about twelve minutes of our play immediately which was a good head-start. The issues were complex and much discussion and research had to be done. We tried to balance the scenes between personal and global and we tried to present conflict issues in ways that audiences could relate to straight away. We also determined that we must keep a sense of humour about it all so that the play did not become a gloomy, despairing plea for peace, but a positive, hopeful demonstration that peace is possible. The humour played a vital role in maintaining that positive stance.

Another stance taken quite early in the process was to establish that the play was a view by young people from Australia. This arose, not from nationalistic fervour, but from some practical discussions about the group's accents. The group was very conscious of the fact that the festival was an international event and that by now we had also been invited to show the play at the United Nations in New York and in other American venues. We did regular voice exercises to try to ensure that we would be understood by Canadian and American audiences. The exercises were not designed to change the sound of anyone's voice but to make their articulation more precise. This led to discussion about the way language usage can create or heal divisions and conflict and to the idea that the easy-going Australian language might be useful in peace negotiations. One of the group joked that if world leaders walked around saying, 'She'll be right, mate' to each other, it would be hard to start a war. This joke led to an hilarious scene that had quite a serious purpose behind it and that also gave a distinctly Australian flavour to our play without making it jingoistic.

When borrowed material was being looked at, I brought in a haunting poem by Dylan Thomas. When we read the poem, 'Being But Men', aloud, the consensus was immediate that we had to have it. The group understanding of where the play was heading was very strong, even in the early workshops, and such unanimous agreement happened often after that.

The one scene that caused us difficulties was 'Territory', in which a number of complex ideas about aggression, appeasement and disarmament were hammered into an abstract visual presentation. The precision of language and movement required within such an emotionally frustrating scene required a lot of analysis and refining. It went through many versions.

I think I would pick *Piece by Piece* having the best structure I have been involved in creating. The play has set-piece scenes that stand on their own and yet the flow of the play appears seamless and perfectly natural. The strong images and punchlines build on each other to form a powerful sub-structure to the throughline of the play. The intellectual arguments are balanced by honest emotions; the global perspective is balanced by the personal experiences revealed. The beginning is surprising, involving and funny and the ending is stirring and hopeful and leaves audiences dramatically satisfied.

This play is a fine example of just how far an achievement by young people can go. At the Festival in Vancouver it played to full houses and a standing ovation at each performance. The United Nations staff were so impressed they made a radio program that was broadcast around the world. But the greatest acclaim came from the other young people at the Festival, some of whom attended every show. At the last performance we asked the 'regulars' as they entered if they would come to the front for the final song and sing along with the cast. They did — they knew all the words — and there were over forty young people joining in the song that finishes, 'Let's all sing together, Sing for peace.' It was a very stirring moment.

Scenario for PIECE BY PIECE

Created and performed by Paul Barrs; Martin Blacker, Tamsyne Fitcher; David Foster, Liz Hill; Kirsty Jordan; Francine Sparre and Justin Wigg, with E. B. as director. Music composed by Martin Blacker. A Shopfront production. Script published by Shopfront.

The play began with an empty stage. The props were lined up along the back in the first scene and this represented the only set. Some costume elements were used, e.g. black tails-coat for the Penguin, white coat for the Scientist, mask for Lion, hats for world leaders. The cast stayed on stage throughout, sitting at the back when not in a scene.

CHAIR	The cast bring on all the props and place them at Back. Kirsty, Paul, Justin and David all place the chair very deliberately, but each in a different spot. They line up to begin the first song and as the guitar starts Liz insists they stop because the chair is in the wrong spot. Some say not to worry about it but Liz attacks their attitude of mediocrity. The argument is loud. Francine asks Liz where the right spot is and Liz says she doesn't know, she just knows that its present place is wrong. More yelling. Martin, unseen, takes the chair right offstage and then announces, 'No chair, no argument'. Everyone accepts this and lines up for the song.
'TOMORROW AND TOMORROW AND TOMORROW'	(From *Macbeth*). The song ends: 'It is a tale, Told by an idiot, full of sound and fury, Signifying nothing'.
	(Note: We chose to start the play with this bleak song and the following bleak scene to establish the depth of the difficulties in seeking peace. The play developed towards greater hope.)
TERRITORY	Kirsty, as Narrator, describes a land where violence is forbidden and where there are no weapons, while the cast lay out strips of green cloth that divide the stage into rectangular blocks of territory. David puts on his Napoleonic hat and becomes a bully. He pushes people off their land saying that he wants it. He puts up no argument, just says, 'I want this land.' The others give in and he takes over three blocks. When Paul puts up some resistance, David punches him. Liz tells David that they could gang up and beat him but they don't want violence so they'll give him the land as long as he agrees not to take more. He shakes hands and agrees. He now has half of all the land. He looks it over with satisfaction as the others move together onto the rest of the land. David then moves to take more land. The others refuse to accept his bullying and lie down in passive protest on the land he wants. He kills them with a stake. A black cloth is laid over them. David moves on to grab more land. Paul decides he must resort to violence but David draws a gun. As David gloats over his victory, the others rush him and take his gun. Liz goes off to throw it in the sea. They cover David in the black cloth and then tie him up with long strips of green material. This black bundle stands there as they argue over what to do with him. Some say let him starve, but then they'd be murderers. Some say build a prison, but he might escape. Some talk about what a nice person he was and how they still do love him. Justin rejects the sentimentality and strangles David. Liz comes back and accuses them all of being murderers. Justin: 'But you've been saved by our murder.' Liz: 'I don't know what we could have done. I just know that what we did do was wrong'. (An echo of the humorous chair situation.) Paul and Martin lift the body on their shoulders and carry him off. The situation is summed up:

Liz: Murder is always wrong.

Paul: It was unfortunate but it was necessary.

Justin: I enjoyed it.

Narrator: And they all lived nervously ever after.

PIECES (A series of very short scenes.) As the others pack up the cloths on stage, Francine does gymnastics. She insists this is her only chance in the play to show off. But she is interfering with the work so Martin carries her to the back.

Language: Liz, at front, gives the Pentagon definition of peace — 'a permanent pre-hostility situation'.

Finger: Kirsty points out that it is a male finger on the button. Everyone then moves forward putting their finger onto an imaginary button as they ask, what if it were a female finger, or a transvestite finger, or — Martin asks very seriously, producing one — a fish finger? They are now all in a semi-circle with fingers on the one button and Kirsty says, 'The horrible reality is, it's a committee finger.' After a sickening grin at the audience, the others go to the back, leaving David.

Third World: David reads an item from a magazine about neglecting the problems of starvation in the Third World — 'Peace is a middle-class concern'.

New Age: Martin sits as a trendy guru and delivers a speech he wrote — 'If peace in the universe can be measured by the length of time between lunch on Sunday, we would find a barbecued watermelon' . . . etc.

Speeches: Justin wonders what stirring speech you could say after a nuclear war. They try, 'Once more unto the breech . . .' etc, and, 'We shall fight on the beaches . . .' etc, but these aren't right. Justin decides it has to be Hamlet's last words, 'The rest is silence'.

THE BALLAD OF THE PENGUIN AND THE LION (Written by E. B. with the cast of Shore Sines. Music by Martin Blacker.) The Penguin is horrified to hear that humans, who don't care about the world, have the power to blow it up. She hits on a simple peace plan. She holds up a sign saying, 'No more war'. She visits world leaders — Gorbachev, Thatcher and Reagan (at the time) — and they all assure her they want peace. Then she meets the Lion and realises that 'all the symbols were getting in the way of people's real wish for peace' and that things are quite complex in the world. The Penguin asks the Lion to 'be king of peace and not of strife'. The Lion eats the Penguin. Everyone marches against the Lion in protest and they all realise then that everyone does want peace so there should be no problem. A Scientist comes forward, holding a model of an atom. (It is a series of light metal bars hanging on a light chain.) She gives it to Francine, telling her this is an atom and 'whatever you do, don't drop it'. Francine is nervous about it and gives it to Justin who also gets nervous and gives it to Paul. As he passes it, the atom falls to the floor. Silence and freeze. 'Now you know the story of how the Penguin became a symbol of peace.'

'BEING BUT MEN' (Song from the poem by Dylan Thomas.) Sung by the boys. The last few lines give the flavour:

That, then, is loveliness, we said,
Children in wonder watching the stars,
Is the aim and the end.
Being but men, we walked into the trees.

FIGHTING (This scene involves a series of arguments followed by solutions, to suggest that there can be solutions to all problems, but the solutions must be worked for, constantly.) As the boys walk away from the front, Paul trips Justin up, laughing at his trick. Justin grabs him and they wrestle. Some of the others cheer the fight on; some try to stop it. David goes to a corner and plays his flute — 'Amazing Grace'. Gradually, all the group go to him and join in the singing. The fight stops and Justin and Paul join the singing. Justin complains that Francine is singing out of tune. She sulks and goes away. Others criticise Justin for being so cruel. Argument. David won't play while they argue. Everyone goes off to a separate spot on the stage. Silent anger. Martin takes a bunch of flowers and gives each of them a flower with a happy greeting. Everyone cheers up. Paul gets his flower last and throws it away, saying, 'Flowers are for girls.' Argument about his sexism. Yelling. Finally, Paul apologises. Martin apologises for starting a fuss about it. They argue about who should be the one to apologise. Everyone joins in as Paul storms away to the back. He picks up a drum and begins a slow steady beat. Kirsty puts a gun (her fingers) to Liz's head. Tamsyne says, 'Don't you threaten her' and puts a gun to Kirsty's head. Rapidly, everyone does the same until there is a circle with a gun at every head. They then all say, 'If you put your gun down first, I'll put mine down.' They decide they will all put the guns down on the count of three. They count on the drum-beat and at 'three' all fire and drop dead. They lie dead while the beat goes on for some time. Finally, Paul says, 'I just keep the beat.' And the drum beats on.

AUSTRALIAN PEACE PLAN Martin suddenly sits up and says, brightly, 'G'day!' He then explains to the audience that Australia has the answer to the world's peace problems in our language and that the group will teach the audience some 'dinky-di' Australian phrases that will set the world on the road to peace. Martin controls the proceedings with a whistle. The group sends up the Australian accent as they teach the audience to say, 'G'day mate!' They then teach the audience to say, 'No worries' and 'Fair dinkum', and offer circumstances for when the phrases should be used. The last phrase is, 'She'll be right, mate'. The examples are outrageous and the final one is a conflict between Reagan and Gorbachev over jelly-beans. 'So, what should they do to prevent nuclear conflagration? They should say what Australians have been saying for centuries. (Whistle.) She'll be right, mate.' Paul then gets each audience member to turn to the person beside them and look into their eyes and say, 'She'll be right, mate'. He assures them, 'That's the Australian peace plan'.

(Note: I'm not usually keen on audience-participation scenes. I believe the performance should stay in the hands of the performers. But in some cases, such as this one, it seems possible to keep firm hold while allowing physical participation by the audience.)

'PIECE BY PIECE' (Words by E.B.) Justin sings this brief, quiet song that says, 'I have to find my own peace Before I point at you.'

IF I HAD A GUN Liz steps forward into a formal speaking position and says, 'If I had a gun and I saw someone cutting the ears off a kitten with a pair of scissors, I'd kill that person. But if I were President of the United States, I would never, ever use nuclear weapons'. Each person has a speech that follows exactly the same pattern. Nuclear nations included at the tail of each speech do change and are: the U.S., the Soviet Union, Britain, France and China. The stories are personal — attacking my mum with an axe; rape; failure in an exam — and establish personal vulnerability which implies that the human beings who have power to kill the whole world might also do that. Martin makes a very funny speech to lighten the scene a little and the scene ends with Tamsyne saying she would kill anyone who embarrassed her and that small countries have no right to embarrass big countries like America. She becomes rather crazed by the idea and Justin tries to get her off. She says, 'You're embarrassing me, Justin'. They freeze.

'THE TYGER'   (Song from the poem by William Blake.) The theme — 'Did he who made the Lamb make thee?'

FRIGHTENED   A brief but chilling scene. David says, 'Look, the important thing about all this peace stuff is that I'm frightened. ' All the others, one by one, say they are too. Martin says, 'I'm not frightened. I'm terrified!'

'NUCLEAR WINTER'   (Words by E.B. from workshop discussion.) The song begins with gloomy descriptions of nuclear winter and repeated chorus of 'Yes, we'll all fall together if they fall.' The song ends with a plea for people to find their 'tender hearts' so no nuclear winter ever occurs. The chorus changes to suggest, 'Yes, let's all sing together, Sing for peace.' The final chorus is repeated over and over with the audience clapping along.

DANCING WITH KANGAROOS

The group and I wasted a great deal of time going through a crash course in all the mistakes a group and director could possibly make in their first playbuilding project, while always feeling the great pressure that we were trying to create the major play for an extensive overseas tour. Some of the early ideas from the group were pretty silly and some of my efforts to nudge them towards deep and intense playbuilding were quite inept. The subject we had chosen — to reveal the soul of Australia to our European audiences — was rather daunting and none of us really knew how to start. The group kept suggesting 'believe-it-or-not' stories about the great outback, while I kept encouraging weird experiments with a kangaroo suit. Out of this strange period we eventually did salvage my kangaroo suit scene, in more sensible form, and a bizarre shark attack scene which popped up in a mad moment of group inspiration. After quite a few workshops, all we knew was that we wanted the play to be a revelation about Australia, that we all loved the name, *Dancing With Kangaroos*, and that all we had were a couple of tentative ideas. We had two major breakthroughs. The first was when I became more methodical and more analytical about the project and led us into a discussion of how to achieve our aim of revealing Australia. The rigour and careful analysis I have written about so much in this book had not existed in the first months of work on this play. This was partly due to the pressures of handling such a huge project with a group fairly new to me — we were trying to raise a lot of money for the tour in this period too — and partly due to laziness. The other play we were creating, *Love Matters*, was going fairly well and I kept telling myself that the group would snap into some ideas for DWK as they saw how good the other play was. I also had a legitimate concern that I should not push too hard on a play that very much needed to be theirs, especially when I had no real idea of where best to push.

When I accepted that we had drifted lazily for too long and that some precision was needed in planning the play, we soon agreed on some basic guidelines. We agreed that the play had to give audiences a certain amount of real information about Australia, so this would be one strand of the play. This led to broad decisions about including life-style material such as the barbecue, the beach and sports. We decided that the best approach to revealing the 'soul' of a country would be through its arts. We thought of making the characters in the play young artists but finally decided to go to the existing arts. We looked to paintings and literature for inspiration. Nolan's 'Ned Kelly' series of paintings provided an obvious image because this captured a folk-hero and an artistic image at the same time. I told the group about the film of C.J. Dennis's *The Sentimental Bloke*, especially the scene in which the Bloke takes Doreen to see a play, *Romeo and Juliet*, and the inevitable clash of cultures ensues with the Bloke yelling for Romeo to 'put in the boot' in the swordfight. The paintings of Russell Drysdale seemed to represent an image of a dry, bare

Australia with his reds and blacks and near-stick figures. These images appealed to and were remembered by a few of us. From him we later took a number of our major images and the basic costume colours of red and black. 'Waltzing Matilda', 'My Country' and something from Henry Lawson were obvious items to include but we were determined to do something with them to make them a bit different.

So, suddenly we had a lot of sensible possibilities for content but still no real idea of what style to use — and no real scenes yet. I asked them to do a barbecue scene because that seemed something easy. They did it well — miming all the props — and there was much clever dialogue. But the thing that impressed me was the social traffic they included amongst the people at the barbecue. That was our second and probably most important breakthrough. I asked them to do the scene without dialogue. They did it and recognised that the actions represented a revelation of the social relationships between these people, especially between the men and women. We then did it a third time and included certain key phrases that were repeated, e.g. as everyone arrived they said, 'G'day.' Some phrases and movements developed into repeated motifs. We included an Italian family and a bludging neighbour and the scene became a quite hilarious revelation of an Australian ritual.

We now had a style — to emphasise movement and social relationships through positioning, with words kept to a minimum — and the hard work became to shape the ideas and material into images that would keep revealing these patterns of behaviour that could be labelled 'Australian'. Many discussions were held on quite minor points, much to the chagrin of some members of the group who were not used to playbuilding. Lengthy and contentious discussions were held about immigration and about the place in our play of Aboriginal Australians. We could not honestly represent Kooris with no-one of that background in the group. But it was also impossible to omit any reference to them. Compromises had to be made. The play had to be about the period of white settlement because it was a play by a group of white Australians. But there were contradictions within the group too. Although most had European and migrant experiences in their immediate backgrounds, some were opposed to further immigration to Australia. There was also resistance from some of the group to having any statement in the play that suggested that Kooris had some special right to the land.

These issues bring up an interesting dilemma for a director as some of the unrefined statements of this group could have been seen as quite racist. How far can a director allow this to go? If a play includes racist, sexist, libellous, or just wrong material, what can you do? In some cases you can bring in a reference book to correct misinformation, you can argue in the hope of convincing the group, or you can withdraw from a project on grounds of conscience. This is hard to do if you begin by saying there are no absolutes. In this case the dilemma for me was resolved through honesty and by sticking to the aims of the project.

I told the group that some of the attitudes being offered could be seen as racist by an audience. We all agreed that we did not want that. We also agreed that we needed to find an honourable way to acknowledge Koori importance, without asking anyone in the group to express political attitudes in which they could not believe. Everyone agreed that we should include an Aboriginal legend as long as it was one that would not offend any Kooris by its use and that would not make political claims with which any of the group disagreed. We used a myth of creation and death from the Tiwi Tribe and illustrated it with a cloth of Tiwi designs. This myth was used alongside the creation story from the Bible, comparing two cultures.

We developed a form of visual ambiguity which gave the play a richness in performance and that solved a number of arguments about presentation of ideas. As long as two or more aspects were present in an image, the group were satisfied. Yet without fully realising it the group found they had created a picture of Australia as a rather brutal and sexist country. And, although they were not all happy about everything that was revealed through the play, they all agreed that the play was true.

The revelations were pretty depressing when we first put the play into a rough structure. This was another turning point. The group did not want to change anything but I convinced them that we needed to show more humorous material as well. We raked through some of the old ideas and gathered a few brief ones that would show a lighter side of the Australian temperament. By threading these into the play we regained a balance that had been lost in our deep involvement with the 'soul' issues.

The final long scene of the play was carefully pieced together over several workshops, working intensely, in much the same way that the long, humorous scenes in *Love Matters* and *Shore Sines* were created. We kept re-working and adding and tightening until a complex picture was created. After giving such a wide-ranging view of Australia, we personified the modern country as a teenage boy with a Dutch mother who is still unsure of himself. He can feel the strength of youth in himself and wants to do something wonderful, if only he can find his real self.

Scenario for DANCING WITH KANGAROOS

Cast and creators — Lynne Atkinson; Andrew Brook; Jamie Campbell; Michael Daly; Melanie Hughes; Nick Jordan; David Malek; Alice Moore; Signa Reddy; David Rendell; Nichole Sullivan; Luke Tebbutt; with E. B. as director. Touring production by Shopfront Theatre.

    The set was five chairs, sturdy enough to stand on, far stage right, and one in the centre back. A variety of props were set out about the stage. The costumes were various combinations of black and red.

'MY COUNTRY' (Poem by Dorothea McKellar.) Andrew, Ziggy and Luke stride to the Centre Front and recite the first few verses — I love a sunburnt country, A land of sweeping plains. . .' etc — as they do they brush away flies. During this, all the others come on very purposefully and take up positions. Lynne carries a furled, red umbrella. Jamie is a Parson and sits at back, darning a sock. David R is in 'country' outfit — long coat, hat. Alice is near him and holds a 'baby', wrapped in a colourful blanket.

DRYSDALE When the poem is finished, the reciters move into positions and a freeze is held to suggest a group portrait in reds and blacks. The Parson sews, pricks himself and says, 'Damn'. Melanie throws a stone to the floor to play hopscotch.

    (Note: Clattering noises on wooden floors — stones, cans, sticks — were a continuing pattern.)

    As Melanie hops the second time, Luke trips her. Mike goes to her, lifts her up roughly, slaps her bottom and hands her to Mum who makes her sit on the floor. Mike kicks the stone away. David M tosses his beer can away and moves to confront David R. They take turns poking each other in the shoulder. Finally, Andrew and Mike rush at the Country Man and hold him. He is bent forward and David M holds his head in both hands, like a football. Nick takes a beer can and sneaks a drink from it. He goes to Luke and circles him, roughing up his hair. Nick grabs Luke and they wrestle. They sprawl to the ground and freeze, Nick with his arm around Luke. Melanie goes to Luke and kisses his forehead. The Parson goes to Nick and lifts him up. He takes the slingshot from Nick's back pocket. He leads Nick to the chair, slapping his bottom as they go. They are face to face and Nick holds out his hand. The Parson gives him the slingshot back. Lynne raises her red umbrella and the three women march sternly across the stage towards Alice. She is afraid. She lets her baby blanket unroll and a bunch of sticks clatter to the floor. Everyone holds a freeze.

    (Note: The only word said in this scene is the first, 'Damn'.)

SELLING AUSTRALIA David R steps forward rapidly, out of his coat, and goes to Luke and Melanie, now characterised as newly-weds. He tries to sell Australia to them with the speedy chatter of a salesman. He has a big map of Australia which they open so the audience can see it. Salesman runs through a lot of facts about Australia, including size, mineral and agricultural wealth, immigration, animals, famous people. While this happens the others begin a small 'orchestra' with sticks, flute and harmonica. Alice sets herself up under a large beach umbrella. She uses the black side of her blanket to cover her head and shoulders so she looks like a Foreign Lady. The humorous Australian Language Song — by David Rendell and Nichole Sullivan — is sung to the newly-weds with much energy and a cute dance routine. The newly-weds insist that they are 'just looking' but they are given free gifts and urged to spend some time at the beach. The Salesman warns them to decide soon, 'I've got a Japanese couple coming over this afternoon.'

TRUE BLUE   As everyone moves into position, David M and Alice sing the 'Hey, True Blue' song — sentimental Aussie stuff — briefly. David is joined by a number of others who form a circle with him, stage left.

THE BEACH   Luke and Melanie lie on beach towels. Lifesavers watch the surf. Andrew comes on and kicks sand in Luke's face, hits him and calls him a poofter. Melanie jumps into Andrew's arms. Andrew goes in the water. The circle uncurls and becomes a Shark with its own humorous theme song as it chases him through the water. Melanie leaps up and down, yelling, 'Shark! Shark!' The Lifesavers leap into action, feeding out line. The Shark opens its jaws to chomp Andrew who screams. Freeze. Luke does a commentary on the scene, telling us who everyone is — including the Foreign Lady on the beach who nobody can see. He shows Andrew how to spray shark repellant in the Shark's mouth but this just makes the Shark cough. They have to bop it on the nose. It races away. Luke shakes Andrew's hand — 'Congratulations, you've just survived a shark attack.' The Lifesavers stand about, punching each other on the chest in bravado fashion. It starts to rain and everyone runs off. David R puts up the red umbrella and tells the audience, 'Australia! Driest continent on earth! But when it rains, it pisses down.'

AEROPLANE JELLY   Only the Foreign Lady is left. She sings the Aeroplane Jelly song. Melanie tap-dances out front, looking nauseatingly cute and holding up packets of the jelly. Others join the song from Backstage.

KANGAROO   During the singing, Luke brings out a kangaroo suit and leaves it laid out on stage. American tourists enter and try to work out what it is. They find it in their guide-books. Luke enters and puts the suit on, which the Tourists find disgusting. As he leaves the Boy tells him he should hop. He does. Lynne comes across the stage with red umbrella up. The Tourists declare she must be an 'e-moo' and run off after her.

NED KELLY   Nick enters holding a flat Ned Kelly helmet mask in front of his face. Only his eyes can be seen through the slit; looking like a Nolan image of Kelly. Stylised movement to and from the mask occurs with all the cast. Finally Luke has it but Lynne kicks him and takes it away, saying, 'I want to be Ned Kelly'. All the others move in and hold the mask, shouting, 'I want to be Ned Kelly.' Freeze. They then break into groups to play at Ned Kelly. Some are Rich People in a carriage; some are Gang; some are Police. The red umbrella is twirled to be the wheels of the carriage. The movement is exaggerated and humorous. After the Police ambush them, Kelly and the Gang escape by threatening to shoot a doll. The cast become themselves and talk about the fun of the game. Nichole has the red umbrella and starts doing a slow dance across the stage. As the others go off, Andrew asks. 'Why do we have to turn criminals into heroes?' David R says, 'We're Australian.'

UMBRELLAS   David M watches Nichole and puts up the beach umbrella and dances too. He gets carried away with it and then is embarrassed when he sees Nichole watching him. She takes the two umbrellas and places them centre stage to form a sort of cubby-house. She then tickles David M and chases him around. They get exhausted by the chasings and lie inside the cubby, close but innocent. The others enter and march round and round them in a circle, chanting, 'Rude. Rude. Rude . . .' As this gets louder, David M takes his umbrella and runs away. Nichole leaves, but glares at them defiantly as she puts her umbrella down.

SPORT   A chant of 'We will, we will — beat you!' is set up, led by Alice. A cheer squad lines up at Front and it is very energetic. Finally, each one holds up a card to spell out A-U-S-T-R-A-L-I-A- GOLD-GOLD-GOLD. They yell the letters out as they leap into the air with them. The signs come down as Nick says, 'We lost again'. A couple say, 'They cheated!'. David R walks along the line collecting his bets in his hat. Luke yells, 'Get yer balls' and hands out different types of balls to some of the group. They form a circle and toss the balls high to each other as they yell numbers and types of sports. This starts the link to the next scene. They hold the balls high and Melanie does some somersaults into the middle of the circle, finishing in the splits.

BETTING   While the others form themselves into different gambling images — poker machines, two-up, lotto, cards — David R in his salesman voice tells about gambling in Australia. In amongst the noise, Mike stands up, holding ticket aloft, and yells, 'I almost won!' He then moves forward and says, 'When I win the lottery . . . ' Everyone sighs.

PROUD   Lynne comes forward and declares, 'I'm proud to be an Australian'. Everyone joins in a chorus that is repeated after each brief statement of pride — 'The weather's great; the beaches are fabulous; it's a beautiful country. ' They extol the literature, the wildlife, the Sydney Opera House, Kylie Minogue (current pop and TV star) — but all with tongue in cheek. Mike says, 'I'm proud to be an Australian because the TV ads say I should be.' Everyone sings a burst of the Bicentennial song, 'Celebration of a nation'. Finally, David R says he doesn't care about being an Australian, but he's glad he's not French.

(Note: That line was changed to 'American' for performances in France.)

B.B.Q.   They scatter to form the barbecue scene. Mike is at the barbie, poking imaginary meat about. Only the beer cans are real in this scene — and the sticks. Ziggy sits at back, chopping salad. Melanie brings sticks to the front, sits on the floor and keeps lighting matches. Each little group that comes in has a similar pattern. Everyone says, 'G'day' at the door. The men kiss Ziggy on the cheek, pat Melanie on the head — she gives them a finger sign — shake hands with Mike saying, 'G'day, mate', and take a beer. The women help Ziggy with the food. Lovers arrive, but after fond pecks, they separate — him to the men, her to the women. The Foreign Family arrive and say, 'Hello'. The Dad pinches Nichole's bottom. Mum is pregnant and goes with Dad to the barbie. He even gives her a beer. But she is soon dragged away by the other women who fuss over her pregnancy. Luke is the Foreign Son, dumped to play with Melanie, who chases him all over the yard and finally wrestles him down and sits on him. Nichole puts the salad out near the barbie. The men all dive for it and she slaps Mike's hand.

When she goes, the men grab the food. The women all say, 'Men!' Luke calls for help but when Mum goes to move, the women stop her and say, 'Kids!' A Neighbour joins the men. Mike tells the audience, 'Bludger!' All the men are introduced — all have names like Bruce and Barry (and Bruno) and all say, 'G'day'. Bruno has learnt to say, 'G'day,' now. The Neighbour points out, 'Beer! Barbie! Bewdy!' They all join him, thumbs up, on 'Bewdy!' and freeze.

VEGETIME   From the back, the girls bounce forward singing the Vegemite Song. They dance their way to the front as the others get ready for the next scene. It is an energetic routine; a copy of the TV advert.

THE SENTIMENTAL BLOKE   Some are now seated, stage right, as if an audience. They watch a performance of *Romeo and Juliet*. Brief excerpts are done in between the verses of C. J. Dennis's poem that tells about the Bloke taking Doreen to see the play. Mike plays the Bloke and he steps out of the action to tell the audience directly about the event — 'Doreen and me had been to see a show.' The Shakespeare is done simply and strongly. During the fight scene, the Bloke yells for Romeo to 'put in the boot!' The scene ends with 'Peanuts or lollies!' called from off-stage.

G'DAY, G'DAY   Jamie sings some of this Aussie jingoistic song — 'G'day, g'day, how ya goin'? What d'ya know? Well strike a light', etc. From off-stage the others join in. Three bring sticks and umbrellas together in the centre. Jamie joins these three as the song ends.

FLAGS   As the four crouch, a large yellow cloth is draped over them so they are completely covered. They look a little like Uluru (Ayers Rock). As the cloth is covering them, 'My Country' is recited. As each 'flag' is now brought out, a chant or poem is used. The flags draped over the mound are — the Pukumani cloth (a cloth printed with designs of Pukumani poles of the Tiwi Aborigines) with noise of sticks; the Union Jack with 'Land of Hope and Glory' the Eureka Stockade flag with chant of 'No licences! No Chinese!'; the Australian flag with 'Advance Australia Fair'; the Land Rights flag with chant of 'What do we want? Land rights!'; the United Nations flag is last. Lynne recites part of the Desiderata — 'You are a child of the universe, no less than the trees and the stars; you have a right to be here' etc — as some of them hold the corners of the yellow cloth and raise it. As they do, the four underneath stand, opening four umbrellas and supporting all the cloths on the umbrellas. They slowly walk off with all the cloths held aloft. Others follow, still reciting the poem. A symbol made from the sticks has been left on the ground; it looks like a curved series of arrow-heads. A few gather to look at it. Nick kicks it apart and walks off. Andrew gathers the sticks carefully and carries them off.

BIBLE AND PUKUMANI   Jamie holds up the Bible and tells a brief version of the creation story. Two hold up the Pukumani cloth and several tell the Tiwi legend about death. If possible, this scene is done in darkness with torches shining on the Bible and on the designs on the Pukumani cloth. As the end of the Tiwi legend is told, the cast get into the positions of the Drysdale scene as at the start of the play. The last line of the speech is, 'Tiwi mythology refers to mainland Australia as the home of the spirit of the dead — the home of the spirit of the dead — the home of the spirit of the dead.'

(Note: In some places it was not possible to have lighting but we still used the torches in the above scene and the impact of high-lighting was still there. Sometimes it was not possible to have an offstage — in most schools for example — and we used a line of chairs, backs to the audience, as a back wall, and the cast would sit there when offstage and make exits to there, plus costume changes, etc. We did need the possibility for David R to go out of sight to make a special costume change, but this was never a major problem.)

DRYSDALE EXPOSURE   A freeze for the red and black 'photograph' again. The Parson pricks his finger, says, 'Damn.' The actions are then exactly the same as in the Drysdale scene. After the dropping of the sticks, this scene develops the repeated actions. Multiple images and actions occur around the stage for most of the rest of the play, with focus on some particular actions. Ziggy approaches different men, by moving close to them. Each rejects her. She moves to the front where Lynne has found a beautiful shell. She gives it to Ziggy. David M says, 'Lesbian!' General movement. We hear the Parson counting his collection. Andrew comes to the front and takes off his shirt. He looks at himself in a mirror, admiring. He gets dressed into a brighter shirt, watching himself all the while. The Parson is shaking hands with his congregation. The little family of Nichole, Mike and Melanie go home to a meal out of plastic bags on plastic plates with plastic knives and forks. Melanie is slapped every now and then by Dad or Mum, who snap, 'Melanie!' at her each time. Alice takes her baby over to stage right and sits humming softly to it. David R leaves her to go off-stage. Luke sits at Front, writing. Nick finds Luke is writing a poem. He makes Luke screw it up and then he fires it out of his slingshot, towards the audience. Nick and Luke go to back. Nick with his arm around Luke's shoulder. They laugh at the Parson, who signals Nick to come to him. They face each other. The Parson tosses Nick a couple of coins. David M makes a football charge down the field. Nick tries to block him and is kneed in the face. He falls to the ground. David M is given a beer. Alice, Nichole, Lynne and Ziggy sing a Henry Lawson poem, 'Faces in the Street' — 'They lie the men who tell us in a loud decisive tone, That want is here a stranger and that misery's unknown . . .' etc. Melanie goes to Nick (still on floor) and tells him how she once saw a group of fairies in the bush; one stood on her hand. Nick scoffs but Luke believes her. Nick, Andrew and David M adopt slingshot-firing poses and aim at her. They then rotate in unison and aim at the Parson, the two women at front, Melanie and then they jump around to aim at the audience. The three boys freeze. Ziggy and Lynne talk about the shell and why it is empty. Ziggy picks up the sticks as they talk. The talk is really about loneliness. As they get to the back, Lynne suggests, 'Perhaps it was always empty.' Ziggy drops the sticks and they clatter on the floor. Mike comes to Front as the Bloke. Lynne and Luke join him as his family. He recites,

'An' I am rich, becos me eyes 'ave seen
The lovelight in the eyes of my Doreen;
An' I am blest, becos me feet 'ave trod
A land 'oo's fields reflect the smile o' God.
Sittin' at ev'nin' in this sunset-land,
Wiv 'er in all the World to 'old me 'and;
A son, to bear me name when I am gone . . .
Livin' an' lovin' — so life mooches on.'

Andrew and David M put up umbrellas. David M is at front, his back to the audience. Nick looks at both and then moves to stand in front of

David M. Nick's arm snakes about David's waist. David punches him viciously and he falls to the floor. Alice dances gently with her baby, humming a lullaby. David R enters from offstage and as he approaches her she says, 'Sshhh.' He comes closer and again she signals for quiet. He swings his arm in a stylised punch to her face. Freeze. Alice walks away. David R grins at the audience, tosses his hat back to Nick, then throws a handful of glitter into the air. He throws off his long coat and he is in a corset with feathers and spangles all over it. He makes a kickjump into the air and begins to dance across the stage as he sings, 'Dum-dum-de-dum, dum-de-dum . . .' etc. He keeps up this strong beat and steps to it across the front of the stage. When he comes back, all the others join him, all facing the audience, all stepping strongly to the beat. Lynne has her red umbrella up. Nick puts on the discarded hat and coat. They dance a number of times to and fro across the stage. As the group continues to dance, several actions occur. Mike stabs Nichole with his plastic knife and she falls down. Mike straddles her and begins to eat her, using the plastic fork. She struggles and calls out, 'Don't eat me.' Jamie stops David M and asks, 'What's your name?' David says, 'Malek.' Jamie repeats the question and David the answer. This happens at intervals. Ziggy knocks Luke down and stands over him, choking him. He yells, at intervals, 'Mum. Don't. Please don't, Mum.' Lynne tries to do some variations to the dance but the others stop until she comes back to the beat. Melanie gathers the sticks and starts making the symbol again at stage left. David R lies down, luxuriously, in the middle of the stage, and, to Mike's harmonica, sings a slow version of 'Waltzing Matilda'. The others join in. The three out front still dance to the same beat. A freeze. Andrew steps forward and says, 'I'm not sure what I am. I'm growing up. I don't know who I am.' The others act as a chorus to his musings. This time they say, 'Yet!' 'Maybe for a hundred years I won't know.' Chorus: 'A thousand.' 'Black Australians have been growing for 40,000 years.' Chorus: 'They know!' 'They know us — the whites. But we don't know them. I'm white and young.' Chorus: 'Two hundred years.' 'I'm Australian but my mother is Dutch. I'm Australian but I'm not sure what that is.' Chorus: 'You'll learn!' Andrew has taken off his shoes and socks and become more casual. Ziggy asks for her flute and Luke brings it as 'Waltzing Matilda' starts again. Ziggy plays a European piece on the flute. Alice and David M do an 'American' dance at back. Jamie and Andrew open umbrellas and give everyone an umbrella. The umbrellas are brightly coloured; the Parson has a black one. There is one Japanese umbrella. Lynne and Nick still dance at front, keeping a steady beat like a metronome. Luke joins Melanie and plays with the symbol but she pushes him away and fixes it up. She is given a box kite and she gets Luke to help her construct it. Andrew comes to the front again with his umbrella 'I'm beautiful but I'm embarrassed to say it.' Chorus: 'Struth!' 'I'm clever but I don't want to boast.' Chorus: 'Show-off!' 'I don't like authority.' Chorus: 'Ned Kelly!' 'I'm honest and down-to-earth.' Chorus: 'Fair dinkum!' Andrew puts on a red clown nose. 'I'm happy and friendly.' Chorus: 'G'day, mate. Owyergoin?' Andrew walks to the chair at back and stands on it as he talks. Jamie drapes the gold cloth over his shoulders. 'I want to be free. I want to own my own home. I won't let anyone push me around.' Chorus: 'I'm an Aussie!' 'I want to open my whole heart but I'm afraid. My country is the most beautiful place on earth but I blush when I say it. I'm growing up. I still don't know who I am.' There is a beat and then everyone holds the umbrellas over their faces. Everyone: 'It's all a joke !' They raise the umbrellas high and roar, 'Waltzing Matilda, waltzing Matilda!' Freeze.

This last scene of *Dancing With Kangaroos* is difficult to describe because all the group had created quite deep and complex characters for themselves and much of the action was happening simultaneously. But they still kept the images clear and focussed. The description here can only suggest the broad events of the scene and a general impression of the moods. It was quite a tour de force of performance as well as creation and quite inspiring to see after going through the hard process of creating it with them.

Audiences also found it quite marvellous, as well as confronting and sometimes puzzling. This play certainly did not settle for easy options. It presented a picture of Australia that was fun, thoughtful, complex and critical. And I think it did occasionally touch the Australian soul.

After our last performances in London, the resident playwright at Greenwich Young People's Theatre — one of the most respected professional theatres for young people in Britain — had a long talk to me about this play. He had been very impressed by the quality, strength and complexity of all the work. He was most intrigued by the fact that the play was so 'theatrically sophisticated' and yet all the kids had clearly understood what they were doing all the time and had been in complete control of the performance. The kids did understand all the complexities of *Dancing With Kangaroos* because the play was theirs. They built it.